SEARCH FOR LIFE'S GLORY, SENSE LIFE'S PAIN

Archbishop William Levada.

May God bless you always.

Maurice Grahnas

November 1998.

SEARCH FOR LIFE'S GLORY, SENSE LIFE'S PAIN

BY MAURICE GRACIAS

Rutledge Books, Inc. Danbury, CT

Copyright© 1998 by Maurice Gracias

ALL RIGHTS RESERVED
Rutledge Books, Inc.
107 Mill Plain Road, Danbury, CT 06811
1-800-278-8533

Manufactured in the United States of America

Library of Congress Catalog Number 97-95683

Cataloging in Publication Data
Gracias, Maurice
   Search for life's glory, sense life's pain

   ISBN: 1-887750-84-3

   1. Personality development.

155.92   97-75683

CONTENTS

DEDICATION xi

A MESSAGE FOR MY READERS xiii

WE EMBARK ON THE JOURNEY OF LIFE'S GLORY
AND LIFE'S PAIN...1

1. THIS CAN BE ME, AND THIS CAN BE YOU 7

   .01 IT IS MY LIFE 9
   .02 EARTHY ME 13
   .03 CONQUERING MYSELF 17
   .04 BELIEVE IN MYSELF 21
   .05 BORN IS THE NEW ME 25
   .06 WEAVING THE FABRIC OF LIFE...31
   .07 JUST CHECKING ON MYSELF 35

2. LOVE AND FRIENDSHIP 39

   .01 THE GRANDEUR OF LOVE 41
   .02 LOVE IS ETERNAL...45
   .03 MOTHER'S LOVE...49
   .04 LOVE IS SHATTERED 53
   .05 A MEASURE OF FRIENDSHIP 57
   .06 FRIENDS ARE PRICELESS..61
   .07 ADMIRERS, WE MUST BE...63
   .08 THE WONDER OF THIS WOMAN 67

3. PARENTAL MAGNIFICENCE 71

.01 The Marvel of Our Parents 73
.02 Leaving the Nest 81
.03 Sadness Strikes Some Parents 85

4. DIVINE PRESENCE CAN MEAN MUCH TO US............89

.01 The Supreme Being 91
.02 God Created Me..95
.03 The Banner of Religion 99
.04 Prayer Brings Us Strength 105
.05 Make Us Kinder, Gentler, Beginning with Me............109

WE CAN TAKE A BREAK IN OUR JOURNEY...... 113

5. FASCINATION FOR US 117

.01 Forever Young 119
.02 Appreciating Others..123
.03 Beauty in the Eye of the Beholder 127
.04 Trust is Paramount..131
.05 The Firsts and the Bests in Life 133

6. PERCEPTIONS OF LIFE 139

.01 NEW BEGINNINGS 141
.02 LANDSCAPES OF LIFE 145
.03 DREAM AND DREAM, AGAIN AND AGAIN 153
.04 THE DANCE OF LIFE...157
.05 INVEST IN LIFE..161
.06 OUR LIFE CAN REACH THE HILLTOP 167
.07 THE DREAM AND THE GLORY 171

7. LIFE'S TANGLES AND WRANGLES....................175

.01 LIFE CAN BE INTRIGUING 177
.02 THE AGONY OF LONELINESS 179
.03 STUNG AND IN PAIN..185
.04 A FRIEND IS DEAD 189
.05 BREAK THE BAD NEWS....................................195
.06 LIFE IS A WAITING GAME 197
.07 DIFFERENCES SHOULD BE A PLUS 201
.08 OUR LIMITATIONS 205
.09 DRAIN THE DREGS OF BITTERNESS AND HATRED 209
.10 TIME IS NOT ON OUR SIDE..............................213

8. WORK FOR MASTERY IN LIFE 217

.01 CAN WE LOVE WORK? 219
.02 MONEY AND ITS POWER....................................223

9. ACHIEVEMENT CAN BE OURS 227

.01 A Life Achieving, Achieving 229
.02 No Guts, No Glory 233
.03 What is Success? 237
.04 Budget for Success 239
.05 Second Best is Not Good Enough 241
.06 Reach for the Stars 245
.07 Take Credit for Your Success 249

10. PEOPLE AROUND US 251

.01 Every Face has a Story 253
.02 Do We Show Gratitude? 257
.03 Be Wary 259
.04 Without a Cause in Life 263
.05 The World of Fine People 267
.06 Some of Our Young Today 271
.07 People, Cultures and Lifestyles 277

11. MAKE BYGONES A TREASURE 287

.01 Remember that Day When 289
.02 A Time to Celebrate 299
.03 At the End of the Day 303
.04 Walk Down Memory Lane 307

CONTENTS

WE ARRIVE AT ONE DESTINATION..........................**309**

ABOUT THE AUTHOR **311**

LOVE IN ITS GLORY

My writings in this book
are dedicated
to
my loving wife, Angela,
and
my equally adorable daughters,
Loretta, Belinda and Marina,

in appreciation of

the encouragement, the support and the caring concern
they four have always so spontaneously given me
in all my many endeavors.
Throughout these years,
they have stood by me and believed in me,
even when I wanted so much of them.
They have worked with me to create and to foster
the richness of life
I have so abundantly drawn upon.
I would not and I could not have done without them.

Maurice Gracias

A MESSAGE FOR MY READERS

This book is for all my friends and my friends-to-be. My expectation is that many of the thoughts, concepts and feelings formulated and recounted by me can be one more depiction of the wonders of Life. For many of my readers, it can be a reassurance of their own life's glory, and at times, their own life's pain. To some others, the book could bring resolve, renewal and reinforcement in life's path, and possibly, even a little comfort and hope to those in need.

The book deals with many human and personal facets. It is not my autobiography. There are, however, glimpses of me in this book. The references in the book to Me are not just to me or seemingly to only me, but, as appropriate to some of us as individuals. The book represents a chapter in my worldly experiences in more than sixty countries I have lived in, worked in or traveled to. The book's contents talk about the world at large, including people whom I have met and known, people whom I have seen, and people I have learned about. I have been fortunate in some of the unmatched opportunities I have had.

Life can be as rich as each of us wants to make it and, above all, works to make it. At every juncture, we can bring newfound strength to every endeavor of ours. Let us do our utmost in pursuit of accomplishment in the goals we set and, from time to time, we re-set for ourselves.

My prayer is that God will bless all those who find in my book a re-affirmation of the positives in their own lives. My prayer is also that God will bless those who even remotely might sense an interest in any message in this book.

Maurice Gracias

July 16, 1997.
Oakland, California,
U.S.A.

Note: Information about the Author is in the concluding pages of this book.

We Embark on the Journey of Life's Glory and Life's Pain

WE EMBARK ON
THE JOURNEY OF
LIFE'S GLORY AND LIFE'S PAIN

For each one of us, life abounds in many facets, some the same, some similar, some so different, some so diverse. Glory in life and the search for it rank among the finest and the noblest of these facets. Pain in everyday life and the sensing of it are among the most dismal, and at times the most enfeebling.

Life is not all glory. Life is not all pain. As we travel through the following pages of this book, we will explore some but not all of the glory and not all of the pain we humans encounter. As we undertake this travel, you and I in our own special way will want to confirm and to better our understanding of the reality and the complexity of life.

Sooner than later, if it appeals to us, let us decide to begin this particular journey in this book, one of the many journeys in life we undertake. If we want to, we can do the journey through this book in stages. We can disembark quite often, as often as we want to, perhaps after each essay or after a selection of essays. As we travel on, we make stops. We deliberate on

You and Me as the person, the individual described as I, and what we might do and should do as we proceed to more closely analyze and identify our own personality. We advance, first to the radiance of the glow and then to the brilliance of the flame of love and friendship. We soon dwell on the magnificence of our parents. Before long, we enter into the realm of divine presence. We move on to the many characteristics of fascination for us. As we journey on, we travel through the gratifying expanse of life and we also come across the rugged terrain in life's landscape. We then face the many tangles and the many wrangles in life, and endure the distress, the hurt and the suffering that can be a part of the elements of our life. At one juncture or another, specifics unique to ourselves come to the forefront and, many a time, we see the glow of the beauty of our own life.

We continue on our journey. We now view our work experience involvement. We reach the triumph of our glory in accomplishments. We see the good and the disappointment in ourselves and in the world around us. We reinforce our feeling that there is so much to achieve in the future. At this juncture station on our journey, before long, we will want to begin to bring back into our life a vivid recall from our own tapestry so intrinsically woven and hanging in memory lane. In this revival, despite our pain, we pledge to discover a time to celebrate our life.

In our lifetime, we all contend with issues, with problems, some major, some we easily overcome and we even conquer. We are confronted with difficulties. We must not agonize unduly over our situations, our seeming lack of remedies and solutions. We must not be overwhelmed by any of this. It is often a matter of choice, and a matter of priority. The connective tissue within us is to be made more vibrant. You and I have achievements. We have success. Rejoice in these. We have to learn from yesterday, live for the glory of today, and we must plan with gladness, excitement and enthusiasm for the tomorrow of our lives.

On our journey of life in this book, we may or may not need a travel guide. We are the decision-makers. We are the planners. We are the pacesetters for ourselves. We have the opportunity to search for and to select the routes that we want to and can take in our life. The journey is not for you only, not for me only. It is for everyone who wants to embark on the voyage of discovery, the voyage of accomplishment. Let us begin with a sense of pride in ourselves, and who we are, and who we want to be. We can all be achievers if we want to.

We have done our planning, and we have left ourselves with flexibility on the length of each sector of our journey with the time intervals involved. As we stand at the departure gate awaiting the takeoff time on our travel, we greet each of our fellow-travelers enthusiastically — God's blessing and happy travel always!

THIS CAN BE ME, AND THIS CAN BE YOU

It Is My Life

It is my life. I have to make it. I can make it. I can make it great in the big outside world or in my own little world. In the course of this there is also the possibility that I can break my life. I can be ruined. I can be devastated. In any prefatory analysis, I am convinced that what I do with my life, what I make of it are largely dependent on me. I believe this. I stand persuaded of the truth in this.

So why not do all of it right, beginning now, regardless of the stage in my life at which I am today? I may be riding high. I may be on the uphill climb. I may be drifting. I may not be as high as I would like to be, or I may be in the sinking depths, the deepest of depths.

First, let me settle down to take stock. How far back can I look or, more importantly, how far back do I need look? What have I done right? What have I done not so right? Where have I faltered? Where have I failed? My review goes on. I applaud my positives and my success. I acknowledge the triumphs that have adorned my life path. But today I am going to concentrate on what more needs to be done. I assess the situation in all its phases, in all its complexities. There are areas that call for close attention. Here, I feel the injury. I see the damage building on me. It can be a daunting task. In all this pain, I must not allow anything to affect the perception of my thinking. My world from this moment onward can be blank. It can be uncharted. It can be open for wide accomplishments. I learn to recognize that the broad picture I see could have been brighter and perhaps abounding more in beautiful, fragrant colors.

Despite this, I rejoice in the past. I abandon the anguish I have known. I still remember some of the ten, twenty and earlier years as if these were yesterday. I should not lament over what is behind me in time. I will not regret the experiences of days gone by. Let me not reflect with remorse on the past, except to the extent that it helps me to recognize the origin and the causes of my failures. I may discover a pattern in this. But each of the failures may have been isolated cases. None of this should dampen my initiative; none of this should be my torture. On the contrary, all this discovery should stimulate my growth and I should learn from the experience.

Maybe now I can travel more often on the constructive path of life. We can all rejoice at our successes, at our triumphs, however small they may be. We would like to multiply these more than a hundredfold. But we have to confront reality. Our scope of activity may have had to be narrow and restricted. There are defeats and disappointments and frustrations astride our path of life. They are part of life's scene. They are portrayed on the canvas we paint on every day of our life. We can recall them, but we must not grieve over them. They must not receive prominence in our life. We must not dwell unduly on the past. We cannot escape the past. We cannot relive our life over again. We cannot make amends for any of the defeats, the disappointments and the frustrations that have come our way. I have been witness to my own humanity and my own fragility. I recognize how vulnerable I am, and how often my strength is on the edge or is dormant. I accept that in all this my focus may not have been in the specific areas of need.

Irrespective of how I stand, or where I stand on life's journey, let me brace anew for vibrant action. Let me scan the horizon. Even if it is dismal and dark, I recall that it is my life, and that I want to have my life within my power to make it glow, and not to break it. I want to empower myself.

At this stage, my resolve is to make it. Within me is a place which remains forever inviolate. No one, no one can gain access to it, unless I want them to. It is in here that I will begin to live the unborn tomorrow. I will not look for a crutch. I am in the search to strengthen the power of positive thinking and to develop a vigorous and persuasive sequence of habitual constructive activity.

I continue to brace for action. I assess all my positives. I discover a well-armored fortress within me. In my path I see some strengths within me, strengths I had ignored or I had belittled. I study my weaknesses, and I convince myself that some of these can be conquered and some have to be lived with, converted if possible to the productive. I have to learn to accept myself, with all my goodness and with all my frailties and with all my limitations. I ask myself why I waited this long to make my life abound in even more posi-tives. I have just now given myself a new sense of purpose. I will be seeking constant reinforcement and recognition. I must be sensitive to cultural patterns, many of which are hallowed by tradition. I must learn to empower myself. In this, I continue to make discoveries anew. My strategies must be practical. I must ask myself five critical questions: Who am I? Where do I want to go? What do I have to do to get there? Who, if anyone, will go with me? Who, if anyone, will reinforce my thinking? In all this, my resolve is to get there, come what may.

For me, life must be an unbelievable dream, not a mysterious nightmare. I need to be fearless to pursue my dreams. Many times, I have to trust my own instincts. I have to carve my very own identity, an identity distinct and positive. I am to muster all my resolve to make my life the way I want it to be. My life can be changed in some ways by as little as a single moment. I can change not only for the better, but in some respects I can change to be among the best, the very best. When the world says to me I cannot, I should say I can. I should do it all.

I now sit back. I have journeyed on. This day has been a tremendous experience for me. I have brought myself under scrutiny in a manner I have never done before. I have gained from the exposure of self that I have conducted. God help me! And help me he will, if I seek him. It is my life. My God gave it to me. I should make my life the very best I can, and I will.

_____

EARTHY ME

E arthy Me! This is you saying it. You are referring to yourself. Your feet are firmly on the ground. You are real, body and flesh. As I look closely at you, I reaffirm beyond doubt that you are real and that you are true. As you appear before me, you give me a stirring message about yourself.

In Earthy Me, you are defined as born and nourished, as natural and elegant and dignified. I see you earthy in all creation's grandeur, in all creation's splendor. In you, I see the ennobling of the Earth. In every way, I see you as so much what I want you to be. You have a remarkable presence. Not only are you beautiful and captivating in your very being, but you exude a presence that makes you so convincingly among God's chosen ones — You are Earthy Me.

You are seen as you really are. You put on no airs. You do not pretend to be what you are not. You are a mystifying you. You are modest and even amazingly, but royally, self-deprecating. You have a refreshing existence. You have an engaging personality. You flood the path of life with a shining light. How wonderful your Creator made you! How you have built on that wonder!

You are earthy. You have the magic, you have the mystique.

You are unpretentious. Throughout the day, you move with graceful informality. You make no claims, implicit or explicit, to worldly distinction that is not in your innermost self. You make no claims to be at the height of worldly fashion or to be trendy in any aspect of life, but you are never outmoded. You do not just seek what is outside of you. You bring forth what you have within yourself. You do not look for self-gratification.

Earthy Me, you are always poised. You are not opinionated. You are not provocative. You wrap yourself in dignity and distinction. In your elegance, you make all this seem so earthy. You do not wear your emotions on your sleeve. You do not portray your vulnerabilities for all to see. You have a disposition to worry, and this is human. You also have a strong tendency not to be consumed by distress and anxiety.

You are Earthy Me. When the burdens you carry chafe your shoulders, and wear you down, you bewitch us with your earthy poise. Without hurt to those around you, you bring them to share with you in your sadness, your disappointments and even in your deprivations. You bring us to respect your tender sensibilities. You will not permit anyone to intrude on your privacy. You never allow all the negatives to overtake you or to drown you. In all this, your composure is to be admired.

Many times your constitution has been jolted. Cracks have appeared in your earthy suit of armor, but in your Earthy Me you do not permit anyone to undermine your confidence or to doubt your capacity for recovery. Your life has been shaped by a repetition of devouring shadows: frustration, less than satisfaction, setbacks, failures and loss. You have not only survived the challenges, you have overcome them, you have been strengthened by them.

You have said that you believe in God. But in the dire circumstances which confront you, at times you have even questioned if God will help. You have had doubts concerning the presence of God in your life. You have resolutely and quietly deliberated. At times, you have felt you have not discovered the truth. You have now put this question behind you, while in your own mode you pursue your sense of the heavenly God. You have concluded that darkness does not last forever. Despite all these barriers, we see so much of tranquility in you. From pain, sadness and grief, you have wrested wisdom. You have shown us that battle scars are not to prevail, and that they do not last forever. Your God is with you.

Earthy Me, even in the most difficult situations, you do not exasperate me. You are not without blemish. Which of us is? Your mind is not scattered. In defiance of the imperfections and life's complexities, you, Earthy Me, are amazing! I acknowledge that you have remained so, in all these years you and I have known each other. Every day we have to answer the call to battle. I admire your strength and your courage, and for this I salute you.

Even when you cry outwardly or are in anger inside you, you do not fail to sport your great smile when you come before those who recognize in you the Earthy Me. Your misty-eyed memories fade into the background. Your wisdom, your talent, your independence, your tolerance, your inner self-containment are all in evidence. You show us a disciplined approach to life.

You are frank, honest and sincere. You are down-to-earth, outspoken without being offensive. In all situations you give the appearance of being in control of your thoughts, your feelings and your actions. At times, we all have to fly against convention, but when you, Earthy Me, do that you do it so convincingly and purposefully that it brings out the best in you. Your gracious earthy bearing belies your fierce determination and your striving for accomplishment.

In moments of joy, you are happier than the humming bird, fleeting from tree branch to tree branch. You are a delight to be with. While all this is happening, you are still Earthy Me, down-to-earth, unaffected overly by life's unpredictable cycles.

In all this, good and bad, you have experienced life with an intensity that sets you apart from so many others. You create your own tradition. You create your own grandeur. We learn from you profound lessons of the cultural enrichment of life. You have an inexhaustible fountain of the love for life. How proud I am of you as Earthy Me! You are priceless, even more priceless than the finest of the world's jewels.

In many facets of life, you give us a message that Paradise is real. Paradise is there for all who want to earn it. You communicate to us that once at the gate we have to learn to continue to work diligently to enter Paradise. Once we enter Paradise we work just as hard. In this pattern, we live in the joys of Paradise. If I could measure near to you, Earthy Me, I would want to be with you in Paradise. In the meantime, let us do all we can to grow in splendor in order to bask in the enduring warmth and sunlight of life's glory.

With all this said, Earthy Me, rejoice in who you are! We are with you, we are in admiration of you! We honor you deep in heart and in spirit. You are awesome in your person and in your beauty and majesty. Stay this way. Earthy Me, preserve always your grace and your splendor. We are blessed to have you with us.

1.03

Conquering Myself

I can be my greatest friend and my best friend, or I can be my enemy, my worst enemy. The choice is unavoidably, but fortunately, mine. The choice is consciously made by me, or is passively thrust on me.

We believe that at birth we were all good and innocent, but that by nature's design we were helpless. We continued somewhat powerless in our early years. Thereafter, we took partial command, and later, in the worldly sense, we took total command of our lives. All through this time, we began and continued the process of directing and programming our lives. We were not necessarily able to contribute entirely or sufficiently to the shape or the form of our life's events or the pattern of our development, and, as a result, of our life cycle.

In this life cycle, good and evil in various degrees occurred. Success and failure also in varying degrees came our way. We hope we all have had more than a fair share of the good and more than a fair share of the success of life.

Life is multifarious and complex, at times beyond imagination, beyond scrutiny, at times frightfully so. Life can be a labor of perseverance and of tedium. Unpredictable scenes can develop. Decisions on choices, options, alternatives or lack of them confront us. Multiple choices are many a time better than no choices. Sometimes we have the time to consider and to ponder over our decisions. At other times we have had to act quickly or instantaneously. Yet, there are other times when decisions for us are not within our realm of activity, possibility or competence. Nevertheless, we must originate ideas and concepts. Innovative measures in implementation can be sought and developed. In this we have to learn not to be overly dependent on other people. Ignorance and lack of knowledge can be damaging and never provide the answer. An element that calls for deliberative thinking plays a role. We come to a recognition that we have to be cognitive strategists. The challenge is compelling.

We will learn that if we do not conquer the negatives in us, life becomes tougher, defeatist and a whole lot less rewarding. At times we are overly in love with ourselves. In this composition of love with ourselves we are unlikely to have much or any competition. Often we feel lost in the maze of the world before us. We see forged the fierce fires of other performances. These fires burn relentlessly, but they should not dissuade us. We are devastated by the magnitude of what lies before us. We cannot control change in the larger context. We stay committed to crucial standards of life that may have distanced themselves from the sometimes real and cruel world of today.

This is when conquering ourselves enters the unbroken expanse in the complexity of life. The scene is repeated again and again in our life, sometimes often during a single day. In our personality, our attitude, our posture, our thought process there can be some not-so-good elements, and even one or more bad elements and features. Some of these negative elements have a tendency to project their ugly heads from time to time. These could emerge from unsubdued jealousy, revenge, vindictiveness, and maybe even evil-mindedness, or maybe from just wanting to be plain difficult or unconcerned without intent to harm others. Again, these could evolve from laziness, from not wanting to be bothered, from lack of confidence in oneself. These come from not having the knowledge to overcome one's deficiencies, from not having the inclination to seek out the knowledge, from fear of the unknown and the uncertain. We must recognize that different needs, different situations demand different solutions. At times, as individuals, we handle seemingly similar situations with very much the same solution. In all this living, under-standing and communicability should gain prominence.

In the quest of conquering ourselves, every one of the negative elements can be overcome if we purposefully take command, heed the battle cry, amass all the forces we can call upon, go into battle, and in the final call of the war for our good we ride high to conquer ourselves. We must know not to over-react or under-react to the issues before us. The struggles and the skirmishes may be many in the beginning, but as we build up our self-conquering armament, the clashes and the opposing impulses will reach a climax and then become fewer. The war against ourselves will be won and Conquering Myself will no longer be an issue too painful, too difficult to contend with, or too obstructionist to gain ascendancy upon. In issues before us, fragmentary decisions can be forged into an interacting complex. We must listen for the signs long before a quiet panic develops. We do all this, and we will soon be in full command. We will become all-conquering, beginning with ourselves.

You and I will be driven by the vision of a single individual, and that individual is You and Me. You and I will expand our horizons. You and I will correct our flaws and our failings. We will not patch them over. You and I will have the choice of a life of most of our dreams or a life of fears. We must dwell on our dreams. We must eliminate all inner conflicts. The inner universe must grow in you and me. Nobody can or should intimidate you and me. You and I are soon to embark on the rewarding journey to conquer ourselves. We are to re-energize ourselves. We can become fiercely competitive with no hurt to anyone around. We will want to conquer ourselves. Be an innovator. Be a creator. In this mode, our inner emblem will be: Conquer Myself. You and I will.

BELIEVE IN MYSELF

I must believe in myself, and with this I am taking the first step on the road to happiness and to success. It does not matter how much others believe in me. It does not matter how much others think well of me or show confidence in me. In the universe around me I will not succeed if I do not have faith in myself, if I do not let the world encounter my strengths.

For all of us, confidence in self is the pre-requisite to success. Many times no one will believe in me, if I do not believe in myself or if others sense that I do not believe in myself. Many times others around us are quick to perceive our lack of confidence in ourselves. At times, they want to see if we are in touch with our feelings.

In the first stride in a new approach to life, bear in mind, that within reason and born of confidence in ourselves, you and I can do most if not all of whatever we, again within reason, venture to do. We can attain whatever we seek to do, whatever we strive to be, again within defined measure. Above all, do not grieve at the talent we do not possess or cannot attain.

We begin by taking stock of ourselves in a serious, honest way. We do not search for reasons to fail, to be defeated, to be overcome. We take the opposite path. We seek out avenues to succeed and to reinforce our thinking as to why we should succeed. You and I build on the attributes we possess. We all have different strengths. Can we embark on identifying them?

All that we do should be seen as an expression of God's creativity in us. Nothing just happens. Everything around us and within us is created. With our zeal and an undaunted purpose, we work and construct on the creation within us.

As we proceed, fears around us swell up in tidal waves of concern, anxiety and hurt. We should not be mired deep into quicksands. We should control emotions, and not allow emotions to control us. Learn to rise above fear of the unknown. We should do all we can to never permit fear to paralyze us. Feel always that we are indestructible. We wonder why we waited so long to make our dreams the reality we want them to be. Remember there is no substitute for success.

You and I present ourselves at our best. We must let shine to the world the beacon of faith which is within each one of us. Exude self-assurance. Do not be modest about our heroics. Be a realist about ourselves. Do not fantasize about who we are or how great we are. Some people can reach heights that others can only dream of.

More than half the battle in life's many ventures is that we should be seen to believe in ourselves. Think Big. Stay away from those who think significantly less than Big. We need to grow not only physically, but emotionally and intellectually. We want to grow with respect for all who are involved with us, and who are or can be affected by our role in life. Soon our world will acclaim us. They will prize you and me. Hope does not exist, unless we believe in it and believe in ourselves. We can believe in ourselves if we develop a record of confronting difficulties, conquering fears and overcoming obstacles. Rewarding opportunities will then be with us. We have to have an enormous sense of ourselves, but not a sense of haughty pride. The aura of self-being should be given possession to create the finest in ourselves, but not to work to our detriment or to the detriment of other people. With this Believing in Myself, you and I are convinced that we are positioned for greatness in our own unique way, but perhaps in the bigger worldly eyes in a small dimension. When you and I believe in ourselves, we empower ourselves in ways that make us grow to confidence and, before long, we find achievement in several directions. Believe in yourself and you will succeed.

1.05

BORN IS THE NEW ME

I t is just past midnight. I have been drifting in and out of sleep. I am lying distracted in bed. For most of the past hour I have been somewhat drowsy, but I am still unable to drop off once again into deep slumber. Somewhat dazed, I stare back at the tireless clock on the nightstand beside my bed. Another five hours must pass before the first signs of daybreak appear, and perhaps five hours and a little more before I rise and begin my day. I am reminded that if I am to fulfill my day's calling and my day's work, I have to wake up and begin my day refreshed, reinvigorated, revitalized and with deep-rooted compulsive convictions.

This can be one more sleepless night to be followed by some pain-choked days. Once again, I make a determined effort to go back to sleep. I just cannot. My mind, my inner being are not at ease. I am tormented. I have a compelling sense of rejection and abandonment. I question the significance and the meaning of life. I dwell over my current situation. I see myself on the brink of mishap, the edge of disaster. I feel betrayed. I feel held hostage. I am torn between the struggle and the despair. I survey the scene hurriedly, and ask myself two questions. Where do I stand in relation to all that is happening around me? What can I do to correct what is not good? I recall my current status, my immediate past, my past since my late teens. I see sadness and gloom. I find so much that has gone wrong in the past, so much that is wrong now. I am knotted in anxiety, in fear. I accede that I am open to attack on several fronts. About all this, I do not think that I am under any illusion. My plight angers me.

I feel insecure. I feel vulnerable. I accept that much, if not all, of my life and its events all these years have had so much to do with me as I find myself today. I may not have attained what I have wanted for myself. How I have planned and conducted myself has not brought me satisfaction. I have had so many desires, so many ambitions and so many goals. Too many of them remain unfulfilled. My material resources are not all that extensive, and this dearth in resources may have held back achievement. But I take consolation in the thought that I possess mental, physical, emotional and spiritual resources which I may not have utilized and, in some cases, maybe I have not even tapped. I lie in bed staring reality in the face. I am lying exhausted in a nightmare, seemingly unable to steer even for the unsatisfying consolation in excuses. I feel overburdened and fearful.

Time marches on. I remain wide awake. I am locked in a struggle. I lie on my stomach as I sometimes do in a predicament. Soon, in my restlessness I roll around and stay on my back. In either position, the vision in my mind is not any different. I try to dismiss from my mind the bleakness and the sadness of my past and my present. Shadows of the ugly and the not-so-pleasant persist. I ask myself whether adversity has a positive place in life. I feel I am slowly walking down the road of despair. I ask myself why an enemy out there can prevail against me. Have obstacles in my life grown, have they been planted or have they emerged from nowhere on my road to happiness and to success? Can this enemy and these obstacles be perhaps only me, not wanting to or not knowing how to overcome difficulties and problems?

Once again, I make a determined attempt to go back to sleep. It is approaching two o'clock. I make a new attempt, and another, and another attempt to re-enter the domain of sleep. I do not succeed. I sink deeper into despair. I make yet another attempt to recollect myself. I am lying in bed brooding over my partly self-imposed helplessness. My life-long personal scenario to succeed in getting into sleep dawns on me and it repeats itself. This scenario has succeeded many times before. In my mind, not so outside my room, I see the sky as a deep rich blue. Superimposed directly ahead of me in the sky are the white, fleecy, icy crystal clouds, with one massive cloud partly imposed on another. In the majesty of the whiteness of the clouds, hundreds and hundreds of white, abundantly woolly sheep are grazing closely huddled together. The sheep converge in all their innocence, unconcerned about anything in the world, painfully for me not even affected in the least about my many cares. How gorgeous nature is! The scene mystifies me. I rejoice in the peace, the tranquility and the composure portrayed by the sheep. All this takes place in the matter of just moments in time. I continue admiring the sheep and their beauty. In the past, for many a year now, as I concentrate on this particular picture of the beauty of creation before me, I have been induced to drop off into deep sleep. But it is not happening this night. I pause again. The sheep remain huddled and cozy among the clouds. I am once again overtaken by the magnitude and the intensity of my concerns.

I lie still for a while. I remain deep in thought. I seem to

27

feel a sense of peace within myself. Suddenly, something remarkable happens. It happens abruptly, unheralded and without warning. I begin to see myself starting anew, yes, starting anew. I pause in my path. The scene repeats itself. I seek courage and resolve. I am wrapped in a feeling of disbelief. A feeling of healthy numbness appears to take possession.

My objectives, my goals short-term and in the longer term are largely the same as they were earlier on, but I begin to think once again on priorities and emphases and on timetables for goals and achievement. I gather new strength. Building anew may seem overwhelming at first. In sifting priorities and emphases I reconcile myself to the fact that some of these may have to go to the back burner. My mind, almost for the first time in a long while, is in a constructive mode. I spend the next two hours and more wide awake, pensive, thoughtful, planning, scheming and dreaming. I begin to see where I may have gone wrong in the past. I will not let the errors of the past, the disappointments of the past, the failures of the past haunt me or deter me. I must put the past into its rightful place. I must not throw caution to the wind. I grow in recognition that time is not always on my side. The time to fix the roof is when the sun is shining.

I have awakened to a new early morning dawn, to a new day, to a new life. A new determination comes upon me. I have to move forward. I have to move on, without carrying the burden of unwanted baggage from the past. I may have to be relentless. I may have to be ruthless, and, in this, I am to make certain that I am not causing harm or injury to those around me.

For me this is a realization that, in relation to some others I know, I have the capacity for much greater strength, much greater courage, doggedness and staying power. I possess more of these attributes than I have given myself credit for. I must untangle the confusion. I must relieve myself of the doubts and the anxieties. I must heal the wounds. My senses are being quickened.

In seeking new heights, I have to be single-minded, self-assured and purposeful. I have to learn that in life there are no problems to stifle us, only opportunities with purpose to spur us on. I have to recognize my opportunities, and I have to pursue them with a relentless passion.

I begin to sense unresolved energy patterns. I become aware that I am not to operate in the bottomless pit, in an apologetic setting. I react to a remarkable evolution in my approach to issues before me. The expansive arena of self-esteem must grow on me. Now, I am not the same person who went to bed six hours earlier. My visit to the future began for me around 4 a.m. today, not long after I repeatedly loved to see the sheep in the clouds. My life will be awash with the blazing sun as it rises. I am mentally, emotionally and spiritually changed. I am re-born. I am re-invigorated. I am refreshed. At this stage, a new, clean, almost flawless carpet with a new challenge lies spread before me. My life is in the process of being reformulated. My goals are to be defined, better defined, with distinguishing characteristics. My individual capacity will make my goals more achievable. Self-esteem, self-worth will enter into my life.

This is the New Me, born and aglow today. I am ready to do battle with the world, come what may. I will not be daunted by the task as being too enormous for me. I must present a cool demeanor. I must get my mind set and re-set in the patterns it should follow for accomplishment. As the sun rises today, I embark on a new voyage with a New Me at the helm. I must be cool and unflappable, even if I am high-strung with plenty of energy. I must learn to keep everything in balance, with a purpose and a perspective, and I will succeed. Succeed I will.

All this or some of what is portrayed in this narration has occurred in some of our lives, perhaps in a somewhat different setting and to a different magnitude. You and I will recall one day, perhaps remember many a time, a night as momentous as this night. We marvel at the advent of your and my deliverance. I was once told that life is a movie. In my life, I am the writer, the producer, the director, the actor and the financier, all rolled into one individual. I may not be at the optimum level in all these roles, and there may be times when I have to rewrite the script, redirect and reassemble for life's performances. All this, you and I will do, and we can do it all in our own personal lives. We soon experience the agony and the ecstasy of being in the forefront. Nevertheless, I should get my mind set on the path I should follow.

As the New Me, I am unique. As the New Me, you are unique. You and I are an irreplaceable, an unrepeatable creation. No one is like you or like me. No one will ever be. We should not live in the shadow of any fellow-being. We will not live in the darkness of defeat, but we will bask in the glory of the magnificence of our individuality and our own selective personality. Born is the New Me for a life full of challenge, with the goal of triumph and of glory. You and I invite others to join us on this voyage to create a resplendent life of our own. Create we will. For each of us, we will build the New Me.

Weaving the Fabric of Life

In his infinite wisdom and goodness, God created millions, billions, trillions and more of humankind. He made us men and women of this world, and when he cast his many molds, he adorned each of us so differently, so uniquely, so distinctively, and with much individuality. As mortals, we sometimes feel that some molds were formed at the end of the day, some early in the newness of the day. Some were less finished than others; at least it appears that way to us mortals. In God's eyes, he made us all equal in most respects, but he endowed us with distinguishing characteristics he gave us as our own.

There came forth from the hand of God one mold, so special that in our mind it outshone others. We are led to believe that from that one mold came forth the special you, the one we most admire. So near perfect was that mold, it had struck as high as a mortal can on a pinnacle. The mold was not to be repeated, not necessarily to be improved upon. Nothing about the mold itself was to be changed. It was God's challenge to you, the particular human being who was brought into this world. Once your presence in the world was accomplished, the mold was destroyed.

We say you are unique because we see so much in you, our loved one, so much which may not be seen in many others or by many others. We look for the skeins that built the weave of your tapestry. You were made in the bounty of your maker's abundance. As a beginning, you were adorned with many seeds of so much that is good and pure and noble. In this mold, your maker did not create another God, but in his goodness he worked specially on the mold. He endowed you magnanimously. He gave you the ingenuity and the opportunity to build on each seed. He set you on the road of life. Onward you march. Rapture, delight, deprivation and tears abound. From all this you wrest new wisdom. You have built, and are building every day a beautiful edifice.

Each day has its difficulties, obstacles and problems for us. Nevertheless, each day has its triumphs. Some are big ones, and many small ones, and, hopefully, maybe these good happenings occur a little more frequently than before. You are building, cheered on by your loved ones.

Your Creator has been and is with you. You have rejoiced in being with him. We revel in this continuing relationship with him. You have not only acknowledged his presence in your life, but you have wanted to be at his side. He knows that you know that in everyday life we all need something and somebody outside of and beyond ourselves, and our Creator can be the greatest of these.

In this journey of life, many among us have to find a niche, and, as we know best, we attempt to fit into the niche we select. A few create a distinguishing niche for themselves. You are one of these select few. You bring us an image that is most engaging. The unique niche that you have created for yourself is ablaze with the glory of your Maker, the glory of humanity, the glory of your beauty of soul, mind, heart and body, the glory of your memories and dreams, the glory of so much that is gracious, kind and gentle. Your affirmation of all that is good, your visionary approach to life, the independence and the creativity in your thinking will bring you even a higher measure of gratification.

The summit of this glory is that every day you add to the wonder and the splendor that is you. Keep building. Our heart is moved with wonder. We want to be with you, to witness and to rejoice in your triumphs. We want to be with you as you weave the tapestry of your life with vibrant colors gleaming. We want to be with you even when less vibrant colors find their place. You have built this special niche. In time you will widen and deepen it to make it even more your own.

We want to tell you this, because we want to thank God for the mold you came from. We want to thank God for the special niche that you have created for yourself. We want to thank God for the near masterpiece he is carving and has carved in you for all of us to be in admiration of. God be praised for giving us You. God be praised, for there abides for now and forever in our memories, all the wonder God has created in You.

JUST CHECKING
ON MYSELF

A ll through life we hear about virtues, about ideals, about living to high and noble standards of conduct and behavior, about moral excellence. We hear about things we should do to foster our own growth, about things we should do to help others to whose advancement we could contribute. As we deliberate on this, we sense that at times we can help others who are less fortunate than ourselves.

Society, culture and history set certain levels of value in life. For many of us we should stop in our tracks to evaluate these value levels. We should ascertain the specifics and the dimensions of the values that concern us.

At various intervals and at different stages in our life, we should check on ourselves on each of the individual virtues, on each of the individual ideals, and on each of the individual standards we value. We cannot check on all. We cannot work on all. We may not have the capacity for all. We should be selective and deal on a priority basis with those that appeal to us most, or those that matter to us most.

I check on my personal life, my career life, my social life, my community responsibilities. I ask myself if I am performing at the appropriate level in several aspects of life in all these sectors. I ask if I am achieving. As always, the presence of success becomes most gratifying. If I detect deficiency, weakness or failure I have to move rapidly in the direction of making amends. I know of different levels of propriety, and I must observe those I have selected.

For example, do I measure up on helping those in need? There are times when we give of ourselves in different areas of activity at no cost to our beneficiaries. At other times, at a professional and skilled level, we will give of ourselves to others, pro bono, at no cost or at a reduced charge. Most often we are conscientious and will not take advantage of someone else's need, someone else's predicament, or someone else's friendship. We realize that what we give of ourselves can, perhaps, be made to go beyond measure.

When I check on myself against the total horizon of virtues, ideals and standards, I see myself wanting in quite a few individual checks on myself. I recognize that I do not do some or all to the highest standards. In some I see myself at the base on the scale. In some I see myself halfway through, or part of the way up. In some I am nearer the top. Our primary objective in striving to action is to reach higher levels. In all this we should learn how to handle failure or, at times, how to live with minimal achievement.

At intervals throughout most of my life, I should check on myself. It will do me good. It will do good to my family and to my community. Corrective measures do good to society, do good to myself as an individual. Let me pursue these matters. I must not stand by silently, seemingly unconcerned at my less-than-proper performance. I must not allow lack of motivation, lack of purpose, and the unwillingness to help win the day.

I must not abandon any of my goals and objectives just because I sense an uphill struggle and a battle which could bring in its wake disappointment and frustration and defeat. I must not spend time on wasteful enterprises. I must not dither. The check on myself should be productive and beneficial to me and to those who may benefit from my activity. All this effort in checking on myself will make me reach closer to the good, and, in time, to the best in life.

LOVE AND FRIENDSHIP

THE GRANDEUR OF LOVE

L ove is the greatest of the great. It is an all-embracing virtue. The grandeur of love cannot be superseded or even equalled. The imposing richness of the word Grandeur cannot be applied with more exquisiteness to any single human attribute except as it relates to Love.

What brings love to this topmost, unequalled peak? It is the fact that, in its best form, true love is at the summit in being genuine, deep and sincere. Love must be reciprocated. It must come from the heart. It comes, not necessarily, with an exact balance for receiving and for giving. In the beginning, one might decide to give, and one might be able to give more than the other gives. It starts in this unequal fashion, but almost always soon attains its best near to its climax. Before long, love is revealing in all its splendor, in all its majesty, in all its grandeur. Inside each of the lovers is a persuasive voice crying out for recognition and for growth.

The grandeur of love begins with a fascination for the party receiving the love. The giver is at the giver's best. True love, continuing true love, brings a whole new dimension to the life of those in love with each other. Joy and happiness can be more rewarding in loving, even more than in being loved. The nobility of love attains its summit when both givers are at their best, and they give in the splendor of all their love.

True love can be all-consuming. It can grow from fascination, from common traits, from shared interests, from talents not necessarily alike, from similar or different attributes. Love can grow from unparalleled concerns or feelings of intentness. Love cannot be induced, it cannot be forcibly given by or secured from another person. It cannot be and should not be enforced. It can be instantaneous on discovery, or it can take root and flourish with time. Love thrives on mutual respect, trust and sincerity. It gives all it can and more, all it has and more.

Love can grow, thrive, prosper and abound if there is reciprocity to the fullest from both. True love holds back nothing. Sharing thoughts, and at times secrets, can lead to deep rapport. Love will not grow to its summit if there is, by either party, a reserve or a holding back, even to the smallest extent. In an unequal scene, one person cannot, and at times, does not give all, when the other gives significantly less than all.

Love is love. Love can become a voyage of discovery, if on your voyage you can search and find the person who you will love the most and who can reciprocate your love. Love is not an infatuation. Love has power — tremendous power. It is fascinating and all-encompassing. It makes us feel good. It makes us feel secure. We should never ignore the radiance of love, or take it lightly or take it for granted. In love you can make a compelling statement without the expression of a single word. You are confident of your intense fondness and your tender feelings. The person loved, girl or boy, young or old, parent or child, is a breath of air as fresh as an early morning blossom, long before the sun beams forth.

In love we manifest a richness of real relationship. We develop a bonding harmony in personality. Many times, the heart has reasons which the mind knows nothing or little about. Love is spontaneous. Love reveals unreleased passion. It brings out the best in each other. It binds together so much good that is within us. Love should not be short-lived. Love should be everlasting. You cannot crowd out the person you love. You cannot become possessive. In true love you are never under siege. Remember that, through the medium of love, your life can be changed in a single, unprepared, unrehearsed moment, even an unsought moment. Not even a predawn hunch can give us a clue of the beauty and the magnificence of love that could greet us on that particular day on the horizon.

True love in its grandeur is enduring. It remains constant, despite all the difficulties, the anxieties, the problems, the uncertainties, the hesitations and the doubts in life. We all know that there are many of these scenes in life. These discouraging events should not damage our love. Before long, the world of romantic discovery begins to enchant us. We communicate in the language of the heart, even in less promising moments.

As we said before, true love can last forever, and contact between lovers must be perpetuated. Does absence make the heart grow fonder, or, some of the time, does absence make the heart wander? There can be truth in both.

Love can be a masterpiece. Love has no rules, no decrees, but love has its price: the greater the love, the higher the price. Nearly all can and do profess to afford the price, but when the price demand is made, not everyone can pay it, even when one wants to. The best in love is not love until you reach the summit and you give it away to someone you admire, someone you honor and you adore. Love should not be lived without the bond of love wrapped in all its glory. In life, we have to love. We have to be lovable. In love it is You and another special person. That makes you both together as one. In the Grandeur of Love, You both together are blessed as One.

———————————————

2.02

LOVE IS ETERNAL

L ove is eternal. Love is beautiful. It is edifying. It is exhilarating. It is always beaming with wonder. It is not a luxury. For us humans, it is a necessity.

Somewhere there is someone you want to be with. A warm and mutually supportive relationship is to develop. Love begins within each of us. Love begins when you feel good about yourself. You can feel good about yourself, whether you look good, portray good in all its forms, or you do this portrayal in a few of its forms. Soon, love leads to adventure along different paths, and one of these is in the life of a person of the opposite sex.

Love is beauty of the soul of each of us. When we have the feel for each other, we bring to each other the closeness of the love in the two of us. Love brings sunshine into the life of our loved one, and in this process we do not block out or limit the sunshine from our own life. The thrust is for outward serenity into life, and for a deep and interdependent relationship.

In life, love makes the difference. We speak of our hopes, our desires, and our dreams. From love comes the support we give each other. In love we face a challenge, many challenges. Shared experiences double, not halve, our joy in life. At the same time shared experiences enable us to face life's burdens and even overcome them. In love we pour out our heart. We bare our soul. We look deep into the eyes of the person we have come to love. The romantic nature of the individual overpowers us and conquers us. Intimacy grows stronger. That person is our friend, and, in time, our best and our greatest friend. We do not feel threatened in any way by our lover. We give respect and we earn respect. With the passage of time, these experiences can be incredibly loving, and so romantic.

A woman has a gentle heart, and men know it. The approval that comes forth from the lover means much more to the woman than all the adoring glances of so many around. Most men and most women will acknowledge this. With her around there is a sense of magic, a sense of music, a sense of rhythm. There is an unforgettable sparkle in her eye. She is eye-filling. She has an imposing physical presence. She is impressionable. Lovers whisper to each other the phantasies of love. There is a prelude to a kiss, an incisive love kiss. The woman wants to feel more powerful, always more attractive, and we should not fault her for this. As love blossoms and grows and grows, she becomes more ravishing every day. Once you have found her, you never want to let her go. She has style. You do not want anyone to compete with her. She has the verve. She is soon a fabulous woman. Love brings out the best in each other. It bewitches both. You both say that your heart raptures for each other. Life takes on a more intimate romance. The mutuality of caring gains prevalence.

Love bedazzles constructively. Love cannot be demanded, it cannot be forced. The girl and the boy look at each other as if there was no one else in the room. Creativity peaks. They awaken within each other two natures and, at times, two fascinations of character. In time, they are entwined. Love grows. Love prospers. Love grows emotionally and intimately. Love creates a wealth of memories. In our love, we have adored, admired, honored each other, and stood by each other in the most difficult situations. We have laughed, rejoiced, disagreed, sighed, sobbed, screamed and even quarrelled. We have recovered from the less encouraging. We work gallantly to regain from all the ills that enter our relationship. Within each of us is a secret enclave which is inviolate. The enclave is sacred to us as individuals. There are times when our lover can enter it. The more often the lover enters into the enclave, the stronger the love is, the more enduring the love becomes. Everything must be done to ensure that the intimacy of love, of relationship, of feeling for or communication with each other is not tainted or damaged. Between you and your lover is a language that only you two speak and only you two understand.

The beauty of love is this. True love at or near the pitch of perfection can be the driving force in all our endeavors. It permeates our mind, our thinking, our spirit, our very being. It can be a compelling force in all of life's works and relations. We cannot be true in our friendship if we have love for others that surpasses our loved one. When we embark on the pursuit of happiness, we devote our efforts to seeking and discovering love, but in our early endeavors often we do not find the love, and we have to continue on our travel. Love at this stage can be our best and most comforting support to cheer us on. In love, there is the pledge of commitment, the pledge of loyalty. All this brings a glow and abiding warmth in our relationship.

Even in the darkest moments of life, love finds a place on the scene for all to see. Sometimes we make decisions with our hearts, not with our minds. Each of these occurrences can be a daunting moment. Love teaches us to give, to share, to yield, to forbear, to sympathize, to sacrifice, to forego. Love cannot bloom, in fact it approaches the end, when one becomes unfeeling, uncaring, unconcerned or little concerned of one's loved one. In the bleakest moments, nothing should be taken for granted, as this may bring ruin to the love relationship. We need to support each other in difficulty and in growth. A realistic task is spread before us. As people we need each other, and when we are working together on a problem, we are not lonely. Love abounds in romance, and we should recall often the great moments of our relationship. Love is at its best when you give the elements of love prominence in the bond that has been established.

The basics of love and intimacy are paramount. They include a magnetic drawing together. They include commitment, fidelity, kindness and an enduring passion. In the intimacy of our love, there is a time for everything, however big, however small, however inconsequential. Love has many moments of infectious glee, at the same time, even the same instant. There is a richness in love which cannot be explained. Love is one of our greatest assets. We treasure love only when we ourselves possess it in all its closeness, in all its intimacy. In love we make our loved one a pearl among pearls. Love is eternal and should always remain prized. We discover that love will conquer all. Love is boundless. The most beautiful world of all is the World of Love. Let each of us make our World of Love, special and unique in every way.

MOTHER'S LOVE

Mother's love always has a special meaning. It is a feeling of deep love, of fondness, of closeness. It is a bonding of an extraordinary connective tissue. It is the gem of the relation between mother and child. In the ultimate, neither party looks for or seeks a single material benefit from the other in this relationship. In true love, both parties only want to give.

A mother gives and gives, and she gives. She never looks back. She makes an exceptionally strong contribution to the lives of her children. Mother's love weaves wonder and magic. Her love abounds in grace and charm and charisma. Mother teaches us that to be at peace and in happiness, we have to accept ourselves, and every day grow to be better.

Mother's love has a special significance. She gives her child love, without the thought of receiving any back immediately or without the child reciprocating too soon. She wants her child to learn, not necessarily to be taught or to be pampered. Mother does not seek anything from her child. She gives life to her child. She gives boundless hope, endless dreams, and much counsel to a receptive child. She gives tenderness, gentleness. For mother these attributes began from her own mother many years ago. They are born of knowledge and of experience in life. They are nurtured in opportunity, in difficulty and in danger.

Mother remains concentrated. She teaches us how to share our success and happiness with those we care about. She demonstrates time and time again that love makes us patient and understanding. Self-indulgence and self-satisfaction are banned as primary from the human relationship. Mother's manner of communication transcends language. The child receives the sense of love, the sense of belonging, the sense of protection and care. The warmth of compassion, the gestures of kindness and the message of love are so strong and so evident. The child knows that mother makes her child strive for excellence.

The child knows mother has cordial deference in conflict. She shows us we can disagree on issues before us, and yet be dignified when we accept a different or a dramatically opposing stand by another. Mother demonstrates to us that life is a series of choices, and that each individual makes these choices and bears the brunt and the consequences of wrong decisions. At times, there are tears. Mother is witness to the time when we are not far from the edge, or in all sadness when we move to the brink once too often.

When difficulties, problems and crises confront us as children or as adults, mother will stand by us when we seek her counsel and her help. She is a stabilizing influence when disturbing situations rear their ugly heads.

We are taught about religion by mother. She teaches us about family life, about our culture, about the good in the world around us. She shows us, as appropriate, the less favorable realities of the world as these elements invade society and take abode in society. She expands our horizons. We learn that there must be a commitment and a dedication in order to win, and that no one should be dragged into the abyss of misery.

In all this, Mother has the support, the encouragement and the compassion from Father who remains endeared to Mother and Child. He is a pillar of strength for both of them, come what may. He helps mother to excel in her role as mother, and provides the reassurance the child seeks. The child learns much from the loving union of Mother and Father. The child observes them sharing responsibilities and burdens, and father making a major or a sizable contribution to all this. They teach their children to be listeners, and to do this with respect, interest and concern. The parents emulate the love that beams forth. The parents want the child to take justifiable self-pride, as the child moves on to earn it. Mother harbors a high level of self-worth, and this characteristic is all the more reinforced in mothers who have achieved significantly in their homelife, in their careers and in all their relationships with the outside world. Mother and father are often very perceptive and very intuitive, and reflect to their children how, in life, acquired and cultivated intelligence can enter the forefront and remain in prominence.

Mother's love offers growth. Mother's love is almost always unconditional. She knows that as children and as growing adults, each day should begin with dreams and dreams. Mother teaches us how we can rise, even when we are struck down. Mother conveys to us how we can build an emotional support system. Sad to say, some mothers do feel used. There are siblings among us who take all they can from mother, and in return give her little or nothing, not even the simple but abiding love of a child for mother.

When all is said, mother's love remains unassailable, both

in its emergence at birth and in the passage of time. We must pour out our heart to our mother. She prays that her children will repeat the good role of the mother, even if the child and the mother are not exactly alike. Mother's love is bandied around us in our culture. With mother, the miracle of love is always waiting for us. Her love remains a beautiful example for all to emulate.

God bless the world for the Mothers he gives us all. Life would be less of a jewel without mother. Life would be less of a jewel without father, without father and mother working together. In their own way, they both teach us to relish life, to enhance life, and in the process to glorify life. Father and mother make an enormous impact on our life. We may not always acknowledge this for all to see. Let us always marvel at them. Remember you choose your friends, but you do not choose your mother or your father. We honor our mother and our father; we revere them. They are among the greatest of God's gifts for us.

LOVE IS SHATTERED

A unit of two people in love at any age is life's greatest relationship, a relationship packed with wonder. In most ties together, love is indestructible. With every passing day, in the best of situations in life, the love grows and it grows. We thrive on this fulfilling relationship, and many, many happy and very happy and the happiest of lives grow. If only all, and I emphasize all, these relationships in wedlock could blossom, and last forever, forever! Many, many may do and do, but sadly some do not. A few generations ago a greater number of love relationships lasted forever than they do today. Some changes in society and in the marriage climate make for a sad commentary on life. Today some marriage relations, many more than they did before, tend to become and do in fact become antagonistic and strained. Marriages do not always remain picture perfect.

In some relationships, let us hope a small number of relationships, at an early stage or between them at a later stage, discord rears its ugly head. The promise and the early wonder do not stay on. Relationships falter. Misinformation and bad communication can hurt badly. Disappointment, blowing of expectations, unreasonable desires and ambitions, frustration and sadness grow from a single incident, or from an accumulation of incidents. Not only do the parties become tense, they become temperamentally intense. The emergence of early signs of a conflict should alert us to the possibility of peril. The relationship begins to open itself to partner hostility.

In a relationship, any one person should not take advantage of the other because in time this factor will destroy the relationship. Personalities get twisted around. Some have entered wedlock blinded and misinformed, unmindful of the realism of life and the always present possibility of conflict. The lovers get emotionally explosive. Unmanaged anger can give rise to harsh words and hurt feelings. In a quarrel, empathetic attention would help. There should be a will-ingness to compromise. Differences of opinion are not respected by either party. We become uncaring. We resort to sharp combative postures. We become hostile. We openly show a lack of feeling for the lovemate. In our daily lives we may probably encounter sarcasm, animosity and hostility, with no gain to either party. We should bring compassion and sensitivity to the forefront, so that the problem can be resolved or placed in the right perspective. Even if righteous indignation is present, it need not dominate the situation or even prevail. We must not abandon the debate on the dream of unity in life.

We must live together, suffer together, or decide to suffer separately. We are forced to choose between self-defeating reaction and aggressive attitudes. There is irritation. We grow out of synchronization. Present are tears and scars. Confusion, hurt and resentment enter. Monologue takes precedence over dialogue. Disillusionment replaces romance. Emotions become volatile. Pain is self-inflicted with little done to confront the issue. Learn to separate the wheat from the chaff. When you have done this, search for the jewels of your love. The beauty of love lies low, and lies damaged. Love is trampled upon. Sometimes there is a pause and a re-assessment. We have to dwell on making concessions, difficult as this may be. A re-grouping may and should result. At other times, sadly, the end is immediate. It is quick. It is destructive. It is total.

It is a pattern of some human behavior to assign blame to others, but any dwelling on this attributing of blame can be self-destructive. We must know when to ignore and when to contest, but the latter must be done constructively. Early on in the tragedy of a lost love, it is time to resolve the various attendant issues so that life can move forward. We must build better communication. Examine the full range of all our alternatives. Evaluate them. Introduce flexibility in the stalemate that has taken abode in the relationship. Is it a case for the treatment of symptoms or the treatment of causes? We must have a feel for indicators and trends. We must not destroy the ultimate bedrock of self-worth that exists in each one's mind.

In all this turmoil, God will identify with us if we turn to him in our need. We know we seek him in the midst of the worst of our concerns, our troubles, our dislike and our hatred of others. We should turn to him with our anxieties of the future. We must remember that God is the one prop every one of us can lean on. In the hour of difficulty, we should not abandon or ignore the best of our friends. The best is our God.

The result of a disappointment in love is a broken heart or two or more broken hearts. There cannot continue to be an unloving relationship between the two. The one consolation is that no one ever died of a broken heart. We must remember this for the two lives and the lives of those immediately affected around them. We can rebuild love if we carefully evaluate the situation, and both parties work on solutions. The virtue of love, the bond of love must not be in the abstract. If the break up in relationship is inevitable, we must take measures of emotional control to preserve in a distinctly different setting a form of love, support and respect built and to be built between the two. Anger, harm and outburst must be defused. Doubt and disapproval must be banished from the scene of the now increasingly distancing relationship.

As our love is shattered, our dreams are shortened. We feel orphaned. We feel abandoned. We have experienced a tragic, poignant ending with one whom we loved so dearly. Each of us languishes in solitude. Let us muster our strength and our resolve, and move on, doing our utmost not to damage the other party or other parties involved, and not to damage ourselves. A strong feeling for the good of our once loved one, respect for our once loved one must never, never be lost. Everything must be done to make certain that love does not vanish into the dark night. For us, even in the misfortune of the shattered love, the greatness of love must not ever fall from grace.

2.05

A MEASURE OF FRIENDSHIP

Two people meet by accident or by design. At this point they can be utter strangers. In most cases the meeting would be uneventful, and soon it could be all over. In some cases in the first or in the early meetings, an acquaintance, may be a friendship of some dimensions begins. It may go beyond the first and the early meetings. It may show signs of blossoming, or it may fade away.

In a very few, very few cases, a certain spark is lit, perhaps within one person, perhaps within both people. What happens next on this developing scene? The sparks within each will begin to burn a little or they will burn brightly, or the sparks will burn well in one, with only a glimmer in the other. In yet other cases, both sparks are quickly, in a short time, extinguished.

The case before us sees a commonality of bond, an appeal of each to the other. They both stand on the threshold of mutual admiration and of friendship. They each recognize that neither is anywhere near or bordering on deity; neither is an angel. Each is human with all the frailties ingrained in or pertaining to humanity. A process is set in motion. There starts to develop a feel for each other's strengths and weaknesses, an immediate recognition that neither one nor the other is all perfect. An

57

attitude of nurturing and of accepting the weaknesses of each other develops, and, strangely, can become the forte of the growing relationship. Opposed to the weaknesses, the strengths of each dominate the scene as the friendship moves on.

A stimulating atmosphere is being created. Do we communicate to those around us the person we are, the person we are becoming? The search and the adventure are on their way. The voyage of discovery begins. It can end soon, may be a little abruptly, or it can continue into the depths, yonder into the distant woods unknown. Early on, the pace of the journey can be different or the same for both parties. It can be a crawl; it can be a gallop. Most times, neither party should throw caution to the winds.

Friendship is not always sexist in its relationship. It can be between the same sexes. It can be with the opposite sex. The finest in friendships has its origin in searches that move to the depths of the soul. The exploration is on the level of the capacity for sincerity, the capacity for trust, the capacity for loyalty. It then proceeds to the capacity for the abiding qualities of head and of heart, and, in appropriate cases, the capacity for love. Personality traits that are embedded in the two parties have to be respected and accepted. Inside each is a sanctuary that never ages. As the search proceeds, the spark that was lit in both hearts at the very start either weakens or burns more fiercely, dependent on the discoveries that both parties make as they together walk through the woods of friendship.

A foundation is laid. The components grow to be firm and rocklike. At this stage it is not now a case of what one can get out of the friendship, but what one can give to the other party, even if the giver is to receive little in return. The depths of the soul between friends are bared to the extent that wisdom dictates this path to both parties. The friendship is on test. Can it survive? Do they want it to survive? In the opposite camp, do they want friendship to flourish? If there is a commitment to be friends and the sparks first lit continue to burn, the friendship will grow.

The friendship of the soul is now moving towards being sealed. These two friends now embark on the adventure into the intellect of each other at levels appropriate to both. Conversation becomes more stimulating. A comfort zone is being set in place. The journey is now less subdued than the exploration of the soul. There is excitement around, maybe in the mind of one or of both. Discoveries can be many. They can give each a thrill. Certain feelings are generated in communication with each other, particularly in the presence of each other. The dialogue grows in richness. There is a rising appreciation of the human greatness in the other.

Cherish friendship. Friendship demands nurturing. We should not over-expect from friendship, particularly in its early days. It is said that friendship is a bank account. We cannot proceed to withdraw and withdraw from the bank account without making deposits and deposits. True friendship, which has stood the test of time and of the ups and the downs of life, has other facets. It influences our outlook on life. In certain aspects the friendship may also mold phases of our life. New visions of possibility loom on the horizon. Sometimes the new world we see is beyond our imagination, but not beyond our hope. We see that friendship can be timeless, and yet so new every day. True friendship does not experience decay and does not succumb to damage.

Friendship enhances our self-worth. Human nature

becomes a treasure house. We try to idolize the best of our friends. We work to emulate the virtues and the qualities of our one friend or of our many friends. We will do all we can to make certain that no harm comes to them. We even see the positive in others who are not our friends. A few good friends, and all of life has a distinctly progressive hue.

Friendship grows from fascination, from common traits, from common concerns, from admiration of another. We continue to grow from an appreciation of the talents and the interests of others. There is a communion between two people.

A friendship, vibrant and strong, not only influences our friendship, but our relationship with others around us. When nothing goes right and proper, when the world is racing by and we are seemingly left behind, that is the time the measure of friendship can attain its peak, if we seek the virtues of our friendship. Friends are wonder-filled people in good times and in not-so-good times. Broaden, widen and deepen your circle. We must build ourself into the best we can, and friends will like us, and, above all, will love us just the way we are. With friendship we must knit the many pieces of life together, and in this we will build a quilt of Friendship of which we can all be proud.

FRIENDS ARE PRICELESS

Who are those who claim to be our Friends, or those we claim to be our Friends? Stop and identify them and what we know about them. We soon discover we have a perception of closeness with most of our friends. Who are the friends we value? We know them; we acknowledge them. Before long, we conclude that some of our friends are priceless.

Among these friends are those who will do the utmost for us. They are by our side in all our trials and in our tribulations. They are with us to rejoice with us in the moments of our triumph. In all we do, they are our support group and more.

Our friends are those around us, those who stand by us. They are those who meet all the specifications and more of a friend, be they our spouse and lover, our children, our parents and our grandparents, our family relatives, our social friends, our work and business associates and our sports acquaintances.

Friends fill us with wonder. We like friends who are receptive to virtues of friendship. They go out of their way to help us in a number of ways. We not only reciprocate their help, but we often help them first. We are around each other when our needs arise, when difficulties confront us. They are there when each of us is unable to help ourselves, or we do not have the time, the skill or the ability to fulfill our needs. They and we are more than friendly in our approach, our behavior, our expression and our manifestation of friendship. They and we step in graciously and make certain that it does not rain on our parade.

We love friends who are secure in who they are and who we are. Both sides must reciprocate. We like friends who have a sense of humor. We like to be around friends who stimulate us by their creative thinking, by their progressive thinking, and by the reinforcement they provide for who we are and what we are. Friends feed off each other's input of sincerity, creativity, knowledge, talent and thinking. In this atmosphere, emotions and feelings of togetherness and helpfulness surface.

As friends, we draw from the basket the best gift of all — each other. We can give our friends and receive from our friends an array of gifts. There is the gift of appreciation for them, and who they present themselves to be, and the greatest of these gifts can be when we relate as friends to each other. For all our friends, in all the problems that surface, we should be the harbor of homecoming and not the one who cannot be beside them in the storm. Focus on the positive, and be thankful for all that we are blessed with. Remember, our Friends are priceless, and they should always remain so.

ADMIRERS, WE MUST BE

L ife would be somewhat dismal if we, humans, did not have admirers, if we did not have people who more than liked us, if we did not have adorers in a modest, sublime sense. There would be less good in life if we did not have with us those who appreciate us, if we did not at times have people in all their sincerity and moderation to honor us. All this self-gratification is human, but it must remain within carefully defined bounds.

Whether it is the beautiful or the not so beautiful, whether it is the powerful or the not so powerful, whether it is those who triumph or who accomplish at different levels, life cannot go on, cannot be ever so rich, cannot be ever so fulfilling without the admirers and the acclaimers around us. As humans, we all love positive attention and, in moderation, we all love acknowledgment.

In all this, it is the beauty of life and its many, many facets and angles that attract our attention. We are told that beauty is in the eye of the beholder. How very true this is! This is where admirers begin. We tend to give some shape and form to our own lives by paying close attention to those we look up to.

What is worthy of my admiration and my acclamation may not be worthy of yours. But no one should despise what others admire, what they acclaim. To each his or her own. It is the individuality in each one of us that gains prominence in our thinking, in our attitude, and in our approach. This is true be it a person, be it a scene of nature, be it a work of art, be it an enunciation of the philosophy of life, be it the proclamation of a new discovery. It does not stop here. It continues whether it be a work achievement, in any shape or form, be it the care we show for others, be it the humility which permeates our life, be it a dedication to a cause. All are worthy of admiration. There is no fantasy in this.

We admire people with brains, with energy, with talent and with skill, and with devotion to their cause. When we admire, we must be sincere, we must be honest, we must genuinely and within us feel a sense of admiration for the other person or thing, in fact, a conviction of the object of our admiration. Too often, we pass by or disregard so many things without an expression of our feeling of admiration. Some of us will not commend or compliment, even when we feel good about others. When we acknowledge the good, we should have a compelling measure of personality in our voice and in our outward expression. We cannot ignore one of the finer facets of human life.

We translate our admiration of an inanimate object, such as a work of art or other achievement, to the human being creating this object of admiration or what it represents. We seek out its creator. At this stage, the creator is in the midst of a foretaste of heaven. Our admirers must commend this and move on.

As humans, we like to be admired, we like to be adored, and we even want to be admired and to be adored. This approval must take place in all modesty. In everyday life we get more than a glimpse of this and more. We can be fascinated by some people. It would be very rewarding to get close to people we admire. Both sides could benefit from this association. So let us do all we can to be Admirers.

The Wonder of this Woman

Here is a woman with a remarkable sense of bearing. She has beauty, grace, style, sparkle and wonderment. She is a woman with charm, personality and warmth. All these qualities are in strong evidence even when she does not consciously want to bring them forth.

She is always superbly mature, always conducting herself responsibly and with a great sense of dignified pride in herself. She is pensive. She is serious. She is never playful. She borders on being an idealist, but not by design or deliberately. She is not jealous about the success of others, or the worldly possessions of others. She never indulges in self-glorification. At the same time, she is not self-deprecating.

A winning personality lives within her. She is amazing in many ways. She is admired, adored and appreciated by her friends. She is one to be cherished. She could be in the presence of her friends, and yet, she, without any expression in words, could communicate convincingly with a precious, select few among those with her.

She is an intelligent conversationalist. She does not talk about other people's lives or of their successes or of their failures.

She is a moderate optimist. Her life has been punctuated with spasms of distress and pain when opportunities that could have come, did not come her way. She remains to a large extent a realist, in the knowledge and the belief that a better and a better day will come. In her subdued optimism, she has no one to cling to and no visible hope to draw upon. The silver lining in the cloud is not yet there for her to see.

Hers is a life story, incredible and yet inspiring. Each time you meet her, you discover a sense of something new, and you begin to appreciate her even more. Each time you see her, she is the splendor, the magnificence of a woman's glory. In her you discover a little seen blend of the essence of idealism and realism.

Once you get to know her, she is warm, friendly and unpretentious. She is not showy, not dressy. She is not a demonstrative person. She keeps her emotions within herself. She is not overbearing. She is attractive. She has a determined flair and appeal. For a person in whom others see so many wonders about her, she is gracious to and understanding of those she respects, values and loves. She never tries to outdo herself. She has few worldly needs and requirements for herself. She does not ask for anything. She makes do with little, and, in some minds, with almost nothing that is fanciful and elaborate. Amidst all this, her imagination and her creativity and her passion for achievement can and do soar to new heights, even heights above those she had set herself earlier.

In the past, indeed for some years, things had not gone well for her. They were not going well in the not so recent past. There was little strong hope on the horizon. Everything seemed doomed. Hope was not with her on a day to day basis, or even in the distance. For all these years, she has had so much less, close to about nothing of the good compared to the lives of her contemporaries. Despite this, she does not seek validation, she does not seek approval. She is not in search of acclaim.

She does not deserve any of the gloom. In all this, she does not show hurt or pain. She does not act emotionally or as one in anguish. She does not even remotely hint at or resort to blaming anyone for her situation, bad as it might be. She is humanly disappointed. She thinks deeply on some of the sad aspects of life, recognizing the reality in everyday living. In these times, she is dejected within, but she is able to admirably contain all this. But the hurt and the disappointment are almost always evident to a discerning friend. However, she is never showing this. She is never frustrated. She remains ever hopeful, even when she is fractured psychologically.

Time goes by and a new day dawns. Her situation changes. She has a new calling. She has a refreshing outlook. She sees hope and adventure on the horizon. She sees certain aspects of self-growth within her grasp. Her thinking is reinforced by her partner in life. He has strengthened her. He may have made her more compelling. He has always been there for her. Many times, we see her resilience unmatched. She journeys on. Armed with all the virtues and the qualities of character and personality she possesses, she moves on to success and later to triumph, a little hesitant at first but resolute in the pursuit of her calling.

In all this, she possesses a sense of drama. In the good sense, she is a driven woman. The splendor of her never yields. She is an unmatched wonder. Her gentle gestures captivate those who know her. She remains gorgeous. We are spontaneously wrapped in her grip. At times, we remain breathless. She is physically graceful and she presents rich images. She is always impeccably groomed. She is fascinating. She is more than interesting, unintentionally captivating our attention. She is always unassuming. At every step you see her reinforce her aura of self-worth.

I stand convinced she is not deity. She does not hold herself out to be anyone but an ordinary being. She is real, living flesh. She is beautiful. She is talented. She is accomplished. She combines intellect with warmth of feeling. She is there for all of us to admire. We remain in awe of her. Her dignity, elegance and grace prevail. The personality she has built dominates the scene. I stand convinced that God did create the wonder of this woman. Every day she is building on this wonder. We are endeared to the personalities of a few people in this world, and for us this woman is among the greatest of these. She makes her friendship so special, so enriching to us. God be blessed for this creation of the Wonder in This Woman.

PARENTAL MAGNIFICENCE

THE MARVEL OF
OUR PARENTS

O ur parents have done so much for us. Life, with all in it at the time, began for us at the moment they brought us into the world. This was the dawning day for us.

For our parents, it was once a new experience to be parents. We were new in this world. They cared for us. In our early days, they provided for our human needs, our material needs, our psychological needs, our spiritual needs. They nourished us by their teachings. They have been there for our emotional needs. They have made sacrifices for us. They have shown strong nurturing instincts. At times, parents have foregone their own necessities and their own comforts in order not to deny their children the joy and the essence of living.

The word 'parents' conjures up images in our mind. Some of these images are that parents exercised an authority over us that was considerate and benign. It is not only the good genes we received from our parents, but all the love and the character they have given us. We grew under their protective wing. They introduced into our lives a particular feeling of pride. They brought a particular feeling of sunshine into new members of the family. They spread the sunshine in which the family basked. Our caring family gave us strength, without which life for us could have been akin to sailing in a rudderless ship.

Years go by from early childhood to adolescence. In our adolescence, our parents have had somewhat less to do for us than they did for us in our early days. We have gained in characteristics of independence in our living and in our growth. At each juncture, they have had a little more time to admire and derive contentment from what they have created in us. They can take time to sit back, and hopefully compliment themselves rightly and in all modesty on their part in building our being.

Our parents rejoice at our successes and our triumphs. They are always there to lend us a hand and to spur us on. They are with us to share in our happiness. They are our advisory counsellors, if we will let them be in this role. They are there to comfort us when problems, setbacks and tragedy come astride in our path. They demonstrate to us how to be stern in appropriate situations, and to be scrupulously fair at all times. They are there to fight our dragons when these monsters rear their ugly heads. They show us never, never to surrender to evil and to wrong.

We recall many images of parents. We see the tender cuddling of the new-born. We see the loving cradling. We see the fond embracing. We see the anxiety and rightful concern for our well-being and for our success. We recognize their saving us from conflict and grief. They teach us fundamentals. They teach us values. They teach us to think, and to exercise prudence. They can demonstrate to us the existence of clashing ideologies, and how we may be able to work around them. They know that we do not know, by mere instinct, many of life's complexities, whether it be understanding situations, whether it be love or support. They know we look for security for ourselves coming from caring and loving parents.

We honor our parents. We even revere them on the worldly scene. We love them, and little by little we learn to do things for them. At times, we do things small, at times more significant things. But, we always aim at the things that give them joy and contentment, and whenever possible give them and us together pride and happiness.

Parents will do most things for their children. From our parents have come more than normal bonding, more than normal growth. They will go to the ends of the earth to fulfill our good and noble goals for us. They will spare no effort. They seem to do the impossible for us. We children reciprocate their love. We cherish them, at times more than we let the world know.

Parents are a tremendous joy to have with us always. They make life so much more fulfilling. They are around when we need them most — in difficult times, in happy times. They show us how to search for solutions. They express love in a thoughtful, caring, endearing way. We should see them as one of our greatest blessings.

Children should never have to live in the shadow of their parents. Everything must be done to promote and strengthen the identity of the child. In all matters between parents and children in the childhood years, a happy balance must be struck between guidance and control, leaning more in the direction of the former than the latter. Parents can be over-protective, with no intent to hurt. Today children are disciplined differently and less disciplined than they were a generation or more earlier. If discipline and the process of raising of the child is in any way adversely affected, there is a danger that development and maturity of children can be stunted, or hampered, with sadly, lasting damage to the children. Parents teach and guide their children to make their own decisions and embolden them to become independent. They repeatedly demonstrate to us that they are genial and understanding. They do not remind children of their past mistakes. They work with their children to build character and to manifest it to everyone's advantage.

For some of us it is awesome to have an overachieving parent, and perhaps doubly awesome, when both parents are overachievers. Overachieving parents should project themselves as role models for their children. They lead them, they provide encouragement and motivation. They can be on the threshold of the children's academic success, their career success, their entire life success. The achievement of the parents and the potential of the young should be held in perspective and be respected. We, the children, must not only survive the over-achievers, we must not only live happily in the bask of their afterglow, but we should enlarge the glow.

There is so much evil in society today, more so than in earlier generations. Every child has exposure to the evil. A child cannot always be prevented from wrongful behavior or wrongful conduct. We cannot program life to avoid wrong. But we can create the environment for each one of us to be guarded against the evil around. There is a program of learning, developing, maturing and consummation of human relations, the process which must take command before long.

Children find that acclaim and praise given in all sincerity can motivate them. Very often children will take kindly to and even accept constructive criticism. At times they will accept rejection of their thinking and their conduct, if these admonitions flow from an abiding and loving relationship with their parents. Children like to have parents who are approachable; parents who will listen and listen. They want parents who will not ignore them, deny them, or reject them. Within reason, parents must reach out to the generation of the young of today. The children want the respect of parents, and the opportunities to reciprocate. Both sides can bring to the other love, joy, gratification and happiness. Both sides can also bring stress, anxiety, disappointment and sorrow.

Many times daughters and sons feel their parents are out of touch with the concerns and the needs of young people growing up in their adolescent days and their adult life. Many times the generation gap, the changes on the social, the cultural and the economic scenes keep apart the thinking and the attitudes of the two parties. This can embitter and destroy the relations between the two generations. Respect for the tender sensibilities of the parties is unintentionally destroyed. In these situations, happy relations can return only if there is an attitude of understanding, an attitude of reconciliation, an embrace of forgiveness flowing from a deep and abiding love. There are no insoluble problems. As time goes on, the offenders — be they parents, be they children — begin hurting from the wrong done to the persons they know and love.

When all is said and done in a confrontation, and time is taken for contemplating and pondering over the issues, there is pain and regret in the eyes of the parents and of their children. At no time are there winners in a battle or in a war between parents and children. This thought must be uppermost in our minds at the outset of an unhappy confrontation. Difficult as this may be, all must work to help everybody win, with no losers. We must focus on the strengths in us, steering away from the dissent that can rear its ominous head too often.

We may have not always been appreciative of our parents. There may have been times when we have not thought the best of our parents, particularly at times when they were firm disciplinarians. We have not approved of them when our thinking ran counter to theirs or was at variance with theirs. There are times when we have sought direction from them. We have sought the attributes of decisiveness. We have learned that in particular situations, it is best to leave some conflicts unresolved.

As we grow up, our parents keep vigil patiently. They observe us struggle with our shortcomings, our setbacks, our frustrations and our failures. They watch us in the knowledge that we may have not experienced a comparable or similar situation before. They see us move along, fall, rise, mature and grow. They see us gain strength, resolve and character, despite our imperfections and our limitations and our newness in the not-so-kind world around. They instill in us an enduring sense of caring for others and for ourselves. They work with us in forging an identity for ourselves. As time goes on, they want to celebrate this identity with us.

Genetically endowed we can be. The root of what we are is found in our parents. As we grow up, we see our parents not only as beacons of love and understanding, but as the light of faith in ourselves and in cultivating faith in others. We always have our parents' love and their counsel. We are cherished as the ones to be worthy to convey the family tradition to this and subsequent generations. We hold to the values our parents taught us. We attempt to emulate the signs and the examples of visionary leadership we learned from them.

PARENTAL MAGNIFICENCE

We must not only love our parents deeply, but we must make them aware of the depth of our love for them. We must make our love for them warm and responsive. We must stand in wonder of them and, hopefully, in amazement of our and their success. To be a parent is to personify and make live forever unconditional love and dedication to our offspring, and, in time, to succeeding offspring.

Above all, we must bear our parents' imprint, good as it is. We can always manifest ourselves to be offsprings mindful of all that our parents have given us. We may not acknowledge it, but our parents taught us profound lessons in so many of the virtues and more than a few of the complexities of life. They instilled pride in us, their children. In our own special way, we must add to ourselves, as proper, a mirror of our parents' personality, their nobility of character, their intelligence and their humanity. We must immortalize them not only within us, but for our own little world and for all the big world to see in children the wonder and the marvel of parenthood.

LEAVING THE NEST

When the special day dawns and children depart their parents' nest, sadness and perhaps a sense of joy envelop both parties. In some cases there is not the desired intermingling of sadness and of joy. The child, married or unmarried, is embarking on a new life as an adult, or is beginning a new student-life or a career-life away from home. It is the start of an adventure.

Much depends on the child. Much depends on the awareness of the situation that each of the parents feel and display. Working together, all concerned can make it a happy event, or, by not working together, a not-so-happy event, even a day to lament. The parents should not succumb in the vacuum of their nest. They should not develop the wrong perceptions of children leaving their nest. They should not be startled by happenings around them in society or their own children's participation in society. The child and the parents should believe in and foster the strengths of care and upbringing. Both sides should guard against problems that may and can arise.

In the child's mind it is the dawn of a new era, something that the child has worked for and has looked forward to. Sometimes, the child is in a kind of a daze. Excitement and perhaps a little apprehension are in the air. It is the start of a life span when there will be no supervision, no regular guidance, little or no instruction or directing, no answering to someone else from an earlier generation. Freedom of behavior, freedom of thinking, freedom to act or not to act, freedom of activity could be frightening to some, but challenging and enterprising to others.

There is nothing wrong in the child having a healthy suspicion about life. This is the day when in reality the young take off their training wheels in exchange for life as an adult. There is nothing wrong in the child unleashing constructively the unlimited but controllable power the parents encouraged the child to develop during the formative years.

The children venture forth in search of the little known and the vast unknown. They can be brave, or they can put on a brave face. The world confronts them in areas they have not been in before, because there was no need for them to go there before. As every day goes by, they develop a recognition that the real world in all its segments and in all its complexities is so different, is more cruel, is more demanding, is more aggressive, is less appreciative than they imagined. Their composure and their confidence are on test.

It is a good world, a beautiful universe, a world full of promise. Yet there is also an ugly side to it. Children should not dampen their enthusiasm and zest for life by letting the less than exciting, the less than challenging, the less than abundantly rewarding in life dominate their thinking. Children should do nothing which will make a defiant display of the character of their independence, whether they have had a successful teenage or they have had years marred by stress. On the contrary, a new blend of interdependence should enter the lives of the parents and the child. They should instinctively seek support from each other as parent and child.

The child, soon moved-in to a new abode, begins to settle in. The feeling of an absent mum and an absent dad enters the thinking, but the impact of this thought should not be allowed to control the child's outlook.

The parents' nest is where the children grew in age, in wisdom, in grace and in character. It is where they first learned their sensitivity and their compassion. It is where they experienced heartbreaks. They should embrace all these elements as a positive, powerful force. They should recognize that the good and the not-so-good experiences are but part of a growth process. We are all the best of friends; we are not just parents and children. Children are among the best futures most parents have.

Let us commend the parents and let us commend the children who leave their parents' nest with a tremendous feeling of all wishing well for one another. The love that brought the child into the world, the love that has permeated their home life and the parent-child relationship over the years, must continue to be full of the best in life, and, if possible, grow stronger in a different context. This is a worthy and a laudable expectation, and a wholesome prayer. It is the beginning of a new expedition in life.

As the children leave the nest, the spirit, the theme, the word, the key and the message that come from parents must continue, in a somewhat dissimilar context, in a different setting with distinctly different emphases. The deeply satisfying relationship of old times must continue, not necessarily with the same priorities. We must remember that a gentle breeze is blowing from the ocean yonder, and that a strong appreciation of the boundaries between parent and child should be always present. We — parent and child — are two different but two similar people. We have different roles in life's relationship. In many ways we are one. Let us preserve together the inner beauty of our nest, the nest we have been in together in all these years. Let us make the beauty, the grace, the excellence of relationship last forever in our lives.

SADNESS STRIKES SOME PARENTS

P arents do not live in an ivory tower. Life is not always a bed of roses. Unfortunately, early for some, much later for others, the serenity of peace and beauty begins to lose its sparkle. There are times when parents are struck by sadness, grief, disappointment and anger. The years of living together, loving each other, the years of learning, discipline, encouragement and working together appear to fade away and vanish into oblivion.

For us, many of the fundamentals of life come from our parents. Among them are love, kindness, forgiveness, thankfulness, humility and pride in oneself. These qualities have to begin within each of us, and they have to become fundamental to family life and to our society. We begin in a small way. Sadness comes to parents who do not see these attributes emerge as some of the cornerstones of their children's lives. At times, the failure is in the parents who have to contend with their own self-esteem, their own qualities. In some cases, this self-esteem may or may not be largely existent or partially existent. The parents may not feel good about themselves. This deficiency in goodness is transmitted to the children. The parents' lives mirror their lack of faith. They are in the throes of dented pride.

The passage of time brings parents to the grip of reality. We do not want to see children self-destruct in any of their ventures. We want to see them display self-confidence, and build and build on this foundation. We show them how to alleviate the tensions that grow from fear of the unknown. We seek divine generosity in the midst of our human needs.

Peer pressure and abandonment of societal values can and do influence the children, more so today than in earlier generations. In our society today teenagers and youth have to contend with pressure points in several forms and in several fields in real life situations. These can include being disrespectful of others, morality lapses, lack of aptitude to develop in all the critical attributes of life, education and training. These can include the evils of violence, sex, drugs and alcohol, and criminal activity in its various dimensions. Parents are called upon to act. But at times scrupulosity and unreasonably rigid enforcement become detrimental to continuing good relations, unless both parties display tact and wisdom. It is when involvement in these areas in a negative fashion builds up that a nightmare grows on us, and becomes a frightening oppression to be dreaded. In society today this phase starts sooner than it did in earlier generations, and it becomes embedded in society with greater intensity. Many children no longer look to parents for answers, and some children do not even seek advice. Children may indulge in stall tactics, and avoid correct and acceptable conduct. At times, parents sense and see, and even experience helplessness and ingratitude. Crippling emotionalism takes abode in the parents' life.

Some parents are very involved in the life of their children.

This can hopefully become a two-way street between parents and children. This involvement can create positive living for some children and parents. It can be destructive for others. Failure produces distress, confusion and turmoil for both sides.

Not all fathers and mothers are role models, great parents or great citizens. Certain parents may have many of the good elements of role models in them, and certain parents may, tragically, have none of the elements. Many are good and ideal parents who have given much to their children, at times at considerable pain and sacrifice to themselves. Some parents will have exhibited patient endurance. The lives of others may be in the depths of ruin or moving towards dismay and destruction. Devastating emotions gain prominence. Sometimes parents cannot give counsel, advice or example to their offspring, because their own lives are in a state of disrepair. The children remain hurt in the process. They become victims of their parents' plight. Destructive erosion makes inroads in the relationship. Sadness comes to these children and to their parents. Both sides dab their tear-filled eyes. There are no winners.

Despondency and futility must not become pervasive. Pain should not dominate our parents' lives. Pain should not be present in the children. The parents deserve better than that. The children deserve better than that. They can all earn a better life; they can all live a better life. The cost attached to suffering must not permeate their lives. Family scorn, public scorn should have no place in the lives of the parents or the lives of their children. We all, children and parents, should work together to ban sadness, grief and disappointments from parent and child relationships in our lives.

DIVINE PRESENCE CAN MEAN MUCH TO US

4.01

THE SUPREME BEING

In order to discover purpose, meaning and fulfillment in life, many of us conclude that we need a Supreme Being to be with us. That Supreme Being is our Creator. Around us is a divinity shaping our lives. We seek strength, courage, knowledge, conviction and support to grow, to mature. Not all of this in sufficient measure is within us, either at the start of our life or as time marches on.

Even if we do not have all we need, we may yet have some of the seeds for what we require to develop. We may have some of the inner strength for this. We must build on this base. The rest, so much of it, must come from God and from those around us, and from the manner in which we participate in life.

Life cannot be fulfilling or complete, unless in his own unique way God is anchored at the center of our life. At times in our life, some of us discover a sense of frustration, a sense of disappointment. Futility enters our life. We grapple. We become despondent. We hesitate. We falter. At times, we know the cause of our plight. At times, we do not. We search for a reason, for an explanation. We may find them all. We may not.

In the right disposition, this is the moment we hasten to search for consolation and for hope. It has been said that we should gather together the burdens of our care, and leave them in the hollow of God's extended hand. God is a giver. He is not a taker. We must not go to him only in distress and in time of dire need, but we should be with him at a time when we have nothing special to ask of him. This thought embodies the value of a friend.

In silence, in peace and in turmoil, we can find God. Most of us do not try to communicate with God except when things go wrong. We then work to brace up our faith and our trust. With this done, we suddenly feel the quieting of the inner storms.

For those who believe in God, God is not far from us. He is in our home. He is in our workplace. He is in our place of fun and pleasure. He is in the streets with us. He is with us when we are with our friends. He is with us when we are with strangers and with our enemies. He can be kindly protective of us if we ask him to be with us.

We can be conscious of God's presence. We can see his fingerprints all around us. We can see his footprints all around us. We stand back and ponder. We pause. We revel in our blessings.

Life is a continuous struggle. Life may cast a shadow on us, but we should not remain standing in the shadow. We must move out into the sunshine of our life. More so than in earlier times, fundamentals and basics are today under a changing emphases. We see sectors of society today reluctant to believe in absolutes in some areas, and in a few or more aspects this is rightly so. No longer does society consider the moral code firm, unflinching, invincible and applicable to all society. On some particular issues, there can be a very volatile perspective observance by some. We are up, we are down. We are on the way up or on the way down or midway there. Life is never stationary, and for us should never be. We need the excitement, the thrill. Much of what is happening around today has never been experienced in civilization before.

At times there is an emptiness within ourselves. We may not find the answers within ourselves. We might even ask which of this emptiness and which of the answers are a message from our God. When we are down, and the count is on, we should remember that God is with us and we should rise from where we are down, and move on. Sadly, too many of us are in search of God only when we are in difficulties or when problems beset our lives. When this happens, we should look to our God to lean on. It is not always to ask God to be on our side. We should be on his side.

If we are believers in the Supreme Being, we begin with the recognition that God is an integral part of our life. God is the center of our life. We value our God. We honor our God. We go to the abode of our God in our need, in our difficulty, in our search for comfort, and most of all we should in our moments of joy and of triumph. We could not have sought a greater blessing in life than in acknowledging our partnership with our Supreme Being. Life is God's grandeur for you and for me. We must build on it, beginning as early as we can.

4.02

GOD CREATED ME

God created Me when there was no Me. I did not come from nowhere. I did not fall from the sky or from a heavenly abode. I did not emerge from the earth. I did not fall out from the dark of the night. The bare truth is this: I was made. I was created by my God.

God placed me on this earth for a defined purpose. He committed to me a specific assignment, an assignment he has not committed to anyone else. God's act in creating me was a deliberate, selective and purposeful act. He endowed me with special and unique attributes of soul and mind and body. He made me special when he brought me into being. He wants me to become special on earth, as I live the life he so graciously and in all his bounty has given me.

For this task he has put within my reach much that is required to become special. He has not given me all; he has not put everything I need within my grasp. He wants me to conceive and develop what is not within me. He wants me to display imagination and creativity. He wants me to work at it. The task is not simple; it is not easy; it cannot be accomplished in a day or in a year. I am to spend a lifetime working on my life plan. I have to see my life grow, and grow and grow to its best, to its peak.

What a blessing he has given me with this opportunity! What I make of it is mine to do. What I do should show me at my finest. I may not accomplish wonders, triumphs or miracles. This thought does not detract me from my desire to accomplish, or to work at growing and achieving.

Let me begin. As a child, as a teenager, as a young adult, as I journey through the middle years, as I grow through the winter of life, the scene around me changes and will always change. My desires, my goals and my ambitions change. As the years go by, the spirituality within me can become more personal, more rewarding if I allow it to.

My responsibilities change. My opportunities change. The best posture for me is to work at masterminding and controlling situations as they arise in life. At times, my sense of achievement will be dampened or moderated in some areas, some critical and vital areas. At times, my sense of achievement will be heightened in some spheres. I will take delight in my accomplishments. I will live with my setbacks, my disappointments, my failures. I accept these as some of life's inevitable chapters. I have to learn to accept them with good grace.

I rejoice in my successes and my triumphs, however small or minuscule they may be in the eyes of the world. I look upon them as not only the pinnacle of my own efforts to become special as God willed it, but also as a vindication of the unique qualities God endowed me with. What pride, what joy, what happiness I discern in all that I have accomplished. I see the signs of God's presence in me, and God's presence beside me.

Life can be enchanting. I know I have to discover and rediscover the deeper meaning of life. How happy all this makes me as I look back in time. I want my Creator to be justifiably proud of me, his creation. I rejoice in the belief that I have done, and I am doing, my very best.

God wants us to feel good about ourselves. What God has made in so many of us is very special. God knows our human limitations. God keeps his promises. We are our own special brand and our own special creation. The world around will accept us for this. We soon come to recognize that the path, the pattern and the realization of God's ways are often beyond our human understanding.

In our lives our greatest tragedy can be to lose God, and, as we go about our lives, not only not know that we have lost God, but not miss him. It has been said that, "What we are at birth is God's gift to us. What we become is our gift to God." Let us make our gift to God worthy of ourselves, and worthy of our creation as a human on our Day One. God will smile on us in all his glory.

THE BANNER
OF RELIGION

Religion has a place in our life. It is a real place, abounding in the noble elements of everyday living. It can be an integral and significant place, if we want it to, if we allow it to. Many a time, without religion we, in our humanity, can be a ship drifting in the ocean of life. Morality, ethics and spirituality defined in proper dimensions can be the backbone of our living. We must foster spirituality in our lives. In the proper sense we, the people, may legislate to some extent about morality and ethics. We can enshrine within us certain unwritten laws on life to honor and to observe. But there is much we cannot do by law, written or unwritten.

Religion can be our guide in good times; and, more so, when the cruelty of the world assails us and when the less kind world makes unceasing demands on us. Religion can be our strength, our reinforcement, and for some our unassailable rock. In all this, religion will not and must not stifle us.

Not too long ago in the days of our earlier generations, and more so with our immediate ancestors, religion played an integral part, a more complete part in our lives.

At one time religion thrived among family clans, almost without question within the clan. Clan loyalty dictated the pattern, and it set the pace. Then, everybody believed in religion, or firmly professed to believe, and no one wanted to face the alternative of being dubbed an outcast. Today, religion in its depth is more the luxury of the firm believers, of the convinced, of those who adhere to traditions and to loyalties.

In earlier times much of life revolved around the churches, the synagogues and the temples. This involved the younger generation, too. In many cultures and societies, our difficulties, our problems, our concerns, our crises and our solutions were discussed with those who ministered to our faith. We sought their advice, their guidance, their comfort. Some of those who ministered to us in the earlier years of this century were a different breed, a cut or several cuts above the ordinary. They were the guardians of our faith, and for some the guardians of our very being. Those who ministered to us in the early days were more knowledgeable of life's complexities than we were, and showed much understanding and compassion. Sometimes those who ministered to us were able to take the ultimate concern and despair away from us, or, at the least, mitigate these problems. They were the forerunners of our psychologists, psychiatrists, psychoanalysts, counsellors, psychotherapists, and more. Today, these professionals provide us help and counselling, but they have not replaced our earlier religious ministers.

Society has undergone a dramatic change in the last five decades, more so in the last two. The pace of change, the content of change, the bounds and intensity of change continue. People are different, the ministers of religion are different. Needs are different and the world is different. We have many good people, we have many good ministers of religion, but the world is not necessarily a better place today than it was fifty or more years before.

All people have undergone a reformation in a windswept, transformed society. Rightly or wrongly, many people are no longer energized by, appreciative of, enlightened by or even tolerant of many religious ministers from different denominations. There are still many ministers of religion who we admire, we honor. But some ministers of religion in different denominations have a very difficult task to manifest, to cultivate, to nurture and to preserve the link with today's society.

The old breed of people and the old breed of religious ministers — both groups in a different world, a different society — are diminishing and fast fading, if too many have not faded away already. Before long the old scene will be extinct, if it is not already burned out. The disappearance of this scene is not a matter of choice. It has been made inevitable by societal changes. The insensitivity of people and, at times, of the religious hierarchy to face squarely today's world has cast shadows at too many levels. All this is sadly fast becoming an accomplished fact spreading into society in all cultures, more in evidence in some nations than in others.

We live in a pluralistic society. Too many among us have gone astray or have lost our way. Life's values have been and are being eroded, more rapidly today than ever before. All around us are indications of more decadence and accelerated decadence. Self-indulgence, moral decline, greed and evil, ethical failures, permissiveness, and a certain sense of liberty are increasingly prevalent in society. They have taken command of society. Many of the youth of today find little or no place for religion in their lives. They have no time for religion. They feel that religion stifles them. The world is in crisis. If those in authority do not take command, the future can become bleak. Despite this, we should not be disheartened or depressed. We must live on, and give religion its place in society.

The non-religious and the religious must share some of the blame for this confusion in life, and also share some of the credit they have earned for the positives. We are a better people in certain respects. In other respects too many of us have sunk into a deteriorating clan, a degenerating clan. For some there is a persistent diminishing of the religious conviction we were raised in, a breakdown in religious life. This large chunk of the worsening among us has not only hurt the laity, but it has hurt the ministers of religion in their role and in their concepts of the world. Some in the position of authority in society are seen to be receding in this most onerous task — the eminence of handling of responsibility and commitment in a new society in today's world.

This authority must re-assess its role, its function, its responsibility. We know that an empire is not necessarily conquered from without; there are empires said to have succumbed to the decay and the abuse from within. We must recognize that in religion and in society there is power, there is peril, there is fulfillment, and, possibly, now a telling failure of the level of our accomplishment of God's mission.

As it always has, religion has today, and more so as we stand on the brink of the twenty-first century, a vital part to play in our lives. It has a crucial, a unique, a satisfying and an enduring role. Religion brings to us a divinity that can fashion and shape our lives. On the journey of life, religion should be in our steering wheel, not in our spare tire.

As we move into the final years of the twentieth century, and will soon enter into the twenty-first century, religion must in no way be mechanical for us. We must work for a deeper spirituality. Religion must not be something we participate in slavishly. Religion is not only for an emergency, but it is for everyday living. Religion is for living in a positive, constructive sense. We should study and learn about religion. We should delve into its deeper meaning. In today's problem-loaded society, the religious hierarchy must counsel and guide us on building ourselves on sound moral principles to formulate our convictions. We should work to study and practice the beauty of religion, for there is a beauty and grace in religion which is not surpassed or repeated elsewhere. Religion need not be overbearing. There must be more open discussions of controversial religious issues. No one should be working with a tunnel vision. In this the people are not asking that, with or without proper debate, the hierarchy should sacrifice or abandon the fundamental principles of religion.

What can religion offer religious worship attendees? What does religion offer those who not only attend religious services, but live their religion every day? Does religion acclaim to them the bounty that life offers? Do we as individuals do enough to make religion an integral part of our lives? Do we, the young and the not-so-young, give God his rightful place in our lives? As in many other activities in life, the outcome is dependent on our participation.

Religion can teach us to derive happiness and sublimity from personal and community prayer. Prayer will guide us into participating in religion, intelligently and with conviction. Religion will tend to not help us if we practice as unintelligible people, as borderline heathens devoid of communication with our creator.

As we said earlier, many of the young are not practitioners

of their religion. We should seek them out, and guide them back. We all know some in different age groups who have good religious tendencies. At times, this is surprisingly rather unusual and uncommon for men and women in their plight, in their age groups, and around their peers. There are those who are openly supportive of our religious attitude and of our deep religious beliefs and practices. In many situations they will speak about religion, sparked by their interest in and their inherent and expressed love for their Creator. These people are known to speak about their faith and their fervent belief in the greatness and in the omnipotence of God. They should receive our support and our encouragement.

We must remember our history and our ancestry. We must be unabashedly, but not slavishly loyal to our religion. Religion is not only the cornerstone of our faith in our Creator, but it is our fortress, our bastion for morality, for ethics and for the good in life, all this so indispensable for honorable living. We proceed from strength in our relationship with God. For some, a new start is to be made. For those for whom religion is a fort, we must continue to secure ourselves in it. For us all, let us begin and renew and reinforce ourselves with God's gift of Faith, and build, and build on this Faith.

PRAYER BRINGS US STRENGTH

In its most solemn and most sublime form, our prayer can be directed to one power and to one authority alone — our God. God loves us. Our focus should be on this God. We are children of a loving God. We can depend on God if we have sincere and trusting faith in him. We need to build on our faith.

Pray to God to grant us humility. We should open our heart and our mind to God's presence and to his infinite love. We have to trust God without fear and without doubt. Soon God will be at work. He will lead us to see his caring hand in our life. With this will begin a feeling of growing trust in our God.

Before long we will enter on a discovery within our inmost self. Let us turn to God. We know you, our God. We want to be secure in God's care. We know that God loves us, and that he cares for us and about us. We do not want a distant God.

If we acknowledge that God is great in our lives, we should be in communion with him. We can do this in one way better than in other ways — by prayer. What is prayer? Prayer is communicating. It takes the form of a continuing demonstrable discourse with God, keeping the channel of friendship with God forever open. The vehicle of this friendship is prayer.

When nothing is going right for us, we tend to ask God why he has forsaken us. This is the moment when we should entrust ourselves into his hands. Even heathens, non-believers, people of little faith will pray to a God in their times of difficulty or turmoil.

We pray to be a stronger person. We ask for powers equal to or greater than life's challenges. We pray when we become a beleaguered people, when we find ourselves besieged. We ask to shake off the despondency within us.

We pray to God that we walk together with him. We pray when we call upon him to honor him and to thank him. We pray when we call upon him for hope, courage, comfort, help and blessing. At this time, he will be at our side or within call.

When we pray we know that power can come and will come from God. As a result, we are not unduly worried, scared, intimidated or anxiety-conscious by what is yet to come. We are undaunted in the comfort of the knowledge that God is on our side, is with us, and will remain with us come what may.

Prayer brings us strength. Is it not time we told God how we really feel? Go into his presence. He will receive us in prayer. Remember the well-known saying: "I asked God for all things that I might enjoy life. He gave me life that I might enjoy all things."

God is my audience. God is my sounding board. All things matter to God. He invites us to put our trust in him. Discover joy in God. All good gifts come to us from our God, be they gifts of our innermost faith, our family, our friends, our moments of joy. Make prayer a part of our everyday life. Prayer comes from the heart. It cannot be bought at any price.

In prayer, acknowledge God's greatness. Thank him for all he has done for us. Ask him to remain at our side always, not to walk ahead of us or behind us, but always alongside us, hand in hand. We walk with him. Remember that in this communicating with him in this way gives us the strength we need and we seek.

MAKE US KINDER, GENTLER, BEGINNING WITH ME

I am not perfect. I am nowhere near perfection. I am nowhere near the best in all things or in many human facets. I am good in some respects, perhaps good in more than an average number of facets that matter in life. I must pledge every day to be in touch with my feelings. I must strive to be a better person.

Is the world today a good place, a better place or a much worse place than it was in the days of earlier generations? Whether it is or it is not, we all have to work to make this world a better place. At times, we feel, we sense the discordance in our lives, in our society. So much of the world could be a better place not only for me, but for many more of us, maybe, ideally for all of us, if not just for me. This can happen if you and you and you and me could ourselves work to make the world a better place than we now discover it to be. In life there is hunger every day: hunger for joy, hunger for happiness, hunger for achievement, hunger for laughter.

Life abounds in mysteries. There is so much that we do not know about, so much that is unknown. The world can be cruel. It can be wicked. In life there is pain every day. Some of this is self-inflicted, some we are individually responsible for. The world must change for the better. It can change. The world must be kinder; it must be gentler. The whole process should begin anew, and, maybe, begin with me and with so many others around me and with you.

Where shall I begin with me? I want to strengthen my moral attributes, my emotional absolutes. I want to add to my characteristics of living right. I want to examine the principles I live by. I want to do my review in considerable detail. I want to travel the road to do better.

Let me rise to the occasion when I can be of assistance in any way to promote what is good, what is noble, what is proper. Let me do my part, even more than my part, if I can. Let me do it with gusto and fervor. This must be the beginning of habit forming.

By my example, by your example, others will change. Little by little our community and the world will become kinder, gentler. It has to begin with Me and all the Mes in the world, and I will be feeling great when I become one strong individual in this group of Mes.

First, let me take care of the negatives in my life. Let me decide situationally that I should not do anything that could border on evil or impropriety, let alone do anything that is evil or improper. I should learn to disagree without being disagreeable. I should learn not to hold others bound in certain areas. I should extend forgiveness. I should not be revengeful. I should be a caring person. I should do all this with grace. Action by each of us motivated by love is one of the most powerful ingredients in life.

Teach me to eschew hatred from my life. Teach me not to judge harshly those around me. We cannot win an argument and in the process not lose a friend. Healing should be a gift I give as often as it is needed, and in the measure it is needed. The providence of God comes to us from events which are a part of our lives and from those around us.

I must sense the humbling realization of life. We must do nothing that may mislead those who associate with us. We want to avoid misinterpretations, misconceptions and misdirection for others. In a pattern of life of not avoiding the bad and the ill, we not only hurt ourselves, but we hurt those who look to us for guidance and example, and even those who may look to us in some respects as role models in their lives.

In all this striving to become kinder and gentler, I must experience and live humility, pride, joy and wonderment. All this most certainly will make me a different person, a better person. Each of us is challenged to leave this world a better place than we find it today, better than when we first came to it. We pray that we all or many, many more of us will accomplish this and become kinder and gentler.

WE CAN TAKE A BREAK IN OUR JOURNEY.....

WE CAN TAKE A BREAK
IN OUR JOURNEY......

We have traveled on, and we may have concluded that there is no person like you or like me, may be in successes, may be in failures, may be in the unattained. In this journey, we have seen some of the adventure in life. In this journey, we may have encountered some of our own experiences of life. As we traveled on, we have heard of the experiences of others. In the course of this travel, we have delved into our Inner Self and reviewed several aspects of Self.

We have moved on. Within each of us, we have the greatest of all virtues in life, and that is what we humans know as Love, in particular the love of and for our dear one, for family members and for friends. Once again, we have been happy to see related to us that our parents are to be honored, to be revered in a worldly sense. We have discussed the relationship between parents and children. We have dwelt on the greatness of God in our worldly abode.

At this stage of our life-travel in this book, it might be best, for some among us, to consider taking one break or a few breaks in between stops, and not to continue the journey without a stopover. As we plod on, we might need this interval and other breaks in our book-travel for as long as we want each of these stops to facilitate our journey. We may feel overwhelmed, distressed or absorbed in what has been related to us. We may need time to give our experiences, our reflections, our feelings more thought. Then, there may be among us those who may not be overly concerned about this travel, and decide to go on with only a short pause.

In our analysis, if we want to, we can travel on, or we can leap clear of the water on our adventure. We can abandon ship if we choose to. Let us make our individual and personal decision. Let us take comfort in whatever decision we ourselves make.

FASCINATION FOR US

Forever Young

Forever Young more than borders on immortality. It emphasizes that when we relate to our fellow beings and when we speak in the spirit of being young, we do not grow old. Growing older, as measured in years lived, is inevitable. For us humans, with the passage of time, the aging process is inescapable. But we must remember that growing older in terms of our approach to life, our attitude to life, our conduct in our affairs are our personal doing, and remaining young can happen to us at any age, be it when we are 20, or 30, or 40 or even later.

Some are old for their age; some are young for their age. Some let growing old grow on them, and they do nothing or little to cultivate or retain a zest for life. Negative patterns of life tug at them and pull them down. They move along the aging path, at times dragging themselves along. They age and deteriorate in everyday living at a much faster pace than their age in years. Not everyone of our friends grows old. Some of them become old by not growing, but by being dragged or tugged through time.

If people are not active — physically, mentally, emotionally and intellectually — there will develop a propensity to age, sometimes almost twice as fast as the count in years. We grow

SEARCH FOR LIFE'S GLORY, SENSE LIFE'S PAIN

old when, again and again, we destroy our ability to discover beauty and excitement in life around us. We know that at any age the future belongs to those who stay young. Recall the adage that a man was said to be 60 years old, but his mind did not know it. He was aiming at being forever young and, better still than this, striving for achievement and gaining on age.

Getting older abounds in mysteries, in illusions, in myths, in misconceptions, in failures to fathom the concept and the reality. Our attitude, our approach to getting older, changes with a better understanding of the phenomenon of getting older. There is an awareness that we have to search for this understanding. This ability to comprehend aging is not easy to come by.

There are many in our society, but not nearly enough of us, who will fight the aging process. We may lose any skill or talent we do not use. Versatility must be one of our strong traits. We must fight old age in the realm of the human spirit, not necessarily the physical process. We are our age today. We do not want to be a day older. Yet we will conjure in our minds an array of life's scenes.

Every young person believes and behaves as if he/she is immortal and hopefully can do no wrong. One way to remain young, even forever young, is to work to search and to adapt the world to ourselves, our emotions, our ambitions, our goals and our pace. This is far from easy. In the adaptation there is give and take, but in no circumstances should we let the world around us take over our lives, or let age deter us in our quest to remain young and live young.

In terms of counting years lived, we are young only once, but youthful strength can and should span many, many years. Work at our goals today, for we will never live this day, today, ever again.   Work at our goals as often as we can;   better still, do it everyday.   Seek the harmony between our body and our mind.

Learn the secret of thinking young. Maturity and experience should not be overlooked, and none of these should be a burden. They should be our assets. Prepare to meet the challenge. We must equip ourselves as quickly as possible with mental and emotional maturity. Accelerate our personal development, a little more or substantially more every day. Keep our healthy lust for life forever thriving.   Bring physical and mental vibrancy into play. Keep our mind active, and keep young our thinking and the direction of our mind. Radiate energy. Infuse personality in our growing up.   Bring to the forefront desire, dedication and resolve.   Do this, and our life will to a large extent fulfill what our dreams desire.

Albert Einstein said, "Imagination is more important than knowledge," and this is particularly true if one wants to be Forever Young. Can we freeze time, so that today's happiness remains forever? No, we cannot.   You and I may be getting older, but we must not get old.   We cannot be 19 or 29 or 49 years of age once again, but we can formulate our life to remain Forever Young.   Years lived, measured in terms of years, months and days, cannot counteract or destroy the beauty or the enormity of being Forever Young.

Age can be chronological.   It can be biological.   It can be psychological.   It can be physical.   Yet it can be made to be significantly or predominantly none of these four.   It can be measured in the wealth of joy and happiness of life, and more of the realism and the triumph that come forth from within us.   This is indeed a complex world.   All through life, when we are young and when we are old, there is a vastness in life's unexplored territory. The adventure awaits us, regardless of our age. Celebrate each moment today. We will not experience that moment again. Stay young gracefully, and we will stay Forever Young.

5.02

APPRECIATING OTHERS

A t times we are so absorbed in life's work, so taken up
with our desires and our goals, so enveloped in our
concerns, so engrossed in ourselves, maybe even
so self-centered that we tend to overlook, and, at times,
unintentionally discount or dismiss the good that there is in
others.

At our creation, each one of us is unique not only in God's
eyes, but our uniqueness becomes more pronounced as we
grow with life's opportunities and life's problems. Our personalities, our attitudes and our relationships are carved,
fashioned and molded by our experiences and by our skills.
The faults and frailties of others, at times less deeper and less
pronounced than ours, become harder to bear, even when we
are riding on the crest of the wave. Often we have to recall to
ourselves that nothing in life is all wrong — even a clock
stopped in its track is recording right twice every single day.

When we meet people we do not like, we acknowledge
even more the good people we know. The serenity and the
courtesy that should always be present in communicating with
each other must be prevalent. We must search out for the good
in others. Look again if you do not find the good the first time
around. Search for the good the second time and the third

time. We cannot fail, if we seek diligently. We must do all we can to bring out the best in our fellow beings. Pause and ask yourself as to how this can be done. Then proceed to do it. There is much that is good. In all this, we recognize that the world cannot have and does not have an overabundance of good.

We must not be jealous of another's well-being, of another's success, of another's triumph, of another's popularity and acclaim. Let not negative notions influence our thinking of that person, our regard for that person, our estimation of that person. That person must be given total, unblemished credit for the good that person is or what that person has achieved. Jealousy grows from a feeling of inferiority, sometimes from a sense of self-deprecation.

Jealousy has only one effect. Many times it does not hurt the person you are jealous of. It hurts you in whom the jealousy is alive. That person will bask in the sunshine of his/her glory, and will move on to greater success, while you remain enveloped in jealousy and brood over something that is unprincipled, unethical and downright wrong and hurtful to oneself and to others. Antagonism and resentment build up as an aftermath or a concomitant of jealousy for the person who harbors jealousy.

Rise above jealousy, antagonism and resentment. Learn to appreciate others. If appreciating others appears not to come easily to you, work hard and diligently at developing in you this quality and ability. Do appreciate others with genuine sincerity. Rewards for you will flow. You will gain, and you will regain and regain a peace of mind that you may have lost. You will go about your own assignments, your own life in a constructive way you have not done before. Continue to appreciate others, and the world will reciprocate. Communications can be spoken, and they can be in silence. Look at all that is positive about people or around people. Often we are impressed by the sincerity and the kindness that is present in the communications coming from others. Your inner-self and your soul will triumph. Remember that there is an attendant challenge in this. We have to recognize all who deserve to be appreciated. We ask that we recognize the greatness of others.

We are told that when we experience bad times, we know what good times are. Similarly, when we meet less likeable people, we know what good people are. Let us begin today, and make the genuine, sincere appreciation of others a positive and distinct part of our personality and of our reputation. In this process we will individually gain much more than anyone else. We will strengthen, and, in some cases, even regain our sense of well-being. When we appreciate others, we can offer to our community much good that is uniquely ours.

BEAUTY IN THE EYE OF THE BEHOLDER

There is an age-old saying that "Beauty is in the eye of the beholder." As we all know, one of the words used in this quotation is demonstrative that this statement is many, many centuries old, perhaps more than ancient. Despite this enormous span of worldly being, Beauty has been in the eye of the beholder from times immemorial to our very day, and this will continue evermore. Down through the centuries and in all civilizations, the saying has remained true, unchanged and unchangeable, while in this time period so much around people has faltered, diminished, been distorted, become extinct and even been misused. Beauty in all its grace and in all its grandeur can be instantaneous in some cases. In other situations, beauty grows with time, magnifies with time.

Beauty is one of God's greatest gifts to humankind and to everything around us. It encompasses so much. Beauty, mostly at first sight, is captivating. It is enchanting. Beauty begins with nature at its best: the extended rich green in the rolling hills amidst impressive scenery, the calmness in the cattle in the barn by the grazing pastures, the majesty of the mountains, the snow-capped panorama of the mountain tops, the gorgeous blue of the sky, the deeper blue of the sea, the crest of the waves breaking on the shore, a few icebergs to strike us in their wonder, the icebergs that advance and recede. We are enveloped in the Beauty as it continues: the teal blue water of the ocean in ever-lasting command, the glory of the sky meeting the majesty of the sea, the gushing rivers, the bridal veil adorning the waterfalls, the stately trees swaying in the strong wind, the soft mellow color and the fragrance of the flowers, and to crown it all the sparkling sunlight in the daylight, and, when night falls, the radiance in the moonlight spreading nature's magnificence for all to delight in from afar. There is more, much more. The beauty remains the majesty of the universe. It will do so in perpetuity. No one, but God himself, could have done all this, could have done so much to bestow Beauty on the world and for his people.

Beauty moves on to the wonderment and splendor of humankind. Beauty has an enormous impact on life. It makes its abode in style and verve, and in the flow of all that it envelops. It is not just an obsession with good works. Beauty begins with the soul. It goes beyond the goodness of the soul. It proceeds to the mind and takes its place in the body. Beauty is not all phys-ical. It can be silent, without audible or loud expression. It can be without outward display. Much of the beauty comes from within the stillness of the heart and the innermost recesses of the mind. It can come from outward self-effacement without the sacrifice of the magnificence of the inner beauty.

Beauty stands out in the presentation that we see in the person or the object before us. It has its origin in our mind. In the next step it proceeds to what is before us. We are all so different, so unique. As individuals we admire or we do not admire the same objects before us. For a few moments, let us admire the beauty of nature and of human success.

The world has the beauty of man's and woman's achievements, so varied, so far-reaching, so all-embracing, so much of our everyday life. To recall a few, there is the magnificence of buildings and bridges, the power of the automobiles, the ships, the trains, the aircraft, the adventure in space, the approach of humanity to animals and to nature, the preservation of the environment, the life protection and lifesaving features of medicine, the brilliance of science, at times the unbelievable and encompassing vastness of the achievements of technology in every endeavor of life. There is more. All this is beauty in its eminence, in all its fineness.

To crown the beauty we have spoken of earlier is the beauty of woman and man — the way they look, the way they feel, the way they relate to each other, the way they conduct themselves in their dealings with each other and with the world around them. Between woman and man in this mode, are sometimes the ambitious and the unattainable expectations which are not given prominence and are not emphasized. These expectations could remain where they should. We also see a more original, primal form of beauty, not distorted by each one's concept of beauty. Beauty forges its own identity. The dream eyes of our lover capture all that is within us. We all need to make this particular form of beauty of woman and man preserve its splendor for eternity and beyond.

As we have said before, beauty is not all physical. Physical beauty is most striking. A woman is graceful. She is elegant. She radiates energy. Her nature is sensitive and she is beaming with goodness. This is all beauty to behold and to celebrate. In its own special way, an emotional connection flourishes between lovers who are attracted by and appreciative of the inner beauty in each other.

In its much broader sense, it is in beauty that we unite with like-minded people. Beauty brings with it the ability to enchant, to attract and to keep together in friendship and in love. Beauty can have its origin in self-love; in many cases beauty grows even greater with self-love and then channels itself into selfless love.

It can be said that beauty is not only in the eye of the beholder, but in the mind of the beholder and in the mind of the beholden. The splendor of creation brings forth the beauty in all things. Without beauty in all its grandeur, life would be shorn of its wonder. Everyday in our life, everyday, we should proclaim from the roof top the greatness and the solemnity of beauty. Sheer beauty gives us so much to behold, so much to marvel at, so much to admire. Beauty becomes monumental. Can we do more in our life to devote energy and to devote more time to glorify the beauty of humanity? We all can, if we pursue diligently this path in life to glorify the Beauty of the beholden by the beholder.

TRUST IS PARAMOUNT

Human relations are based on Trust. We begin with trust, trust in our individual self. It moves on to trust in our spouse and in the family. It proceeds to trust in those around us, to trust in the community at large. Trust is one persuasive component of all human relations. Trust is one of the steadfast pillars on which a personal relationship, a business relationship, a social relationship and a community relationship are founded.

If trust is not present at the outset between two parties, or if it cannot be created instantaneously or with some degree of rapidity, the prospects for a successful relationship are dimmed, and at times even extinguished. An essential ingredient in the discourse to be established becomes absent. Trust has to be introduced in our dealings, almost to the point of saying that it should be injected into the relationship at the outset, and thereafter everything should be done on a continuing basis to promote and to foster alive that trust.

Trust should have its foundation in the paramountcy of sincerity and of truth. Trust depends on good relations and compatibility. Not only can we not shade the truth, because not only is this not right and proper, but the shading can come back to haunt us. We have to be open and sensitive with those around us.

In an effort to win trust, we should not have recourse to flattery. Flattery corrupts and condemns both the receiver and the giver, and is more damaging to the giver than the receiver. Proper approval, proper commendation, proper praise not flattery, can be one of the backbones of human relationship, a compelling backbone of trusting.

Once trust has been established between two parties, we should do all we can to make trust remain alive, grow and flourish. Once trust is in being, reinforce it by feeling and by word and by deed. High integrity has to be in evidence. Sometimes all but one of the components, and that is trust, are present in a relationship, in a transaction, in a deal. The absence of trust between the parties should not be the missing component in any activity. It is tragic to witness a failure for want of trust. There is tyranny in the distance growing from separating the trust and the negative in a relationship. We should work consistently to stimulate a vibrant desire to create and to maintain trust.

We should always be aware that an important ingredient in any human relationship remains the creation and the preservation of Trust. We should not attempt to live without it. We know that trust and sheer gullibility are not the same. We must distinguish between these two. We must remember that we cannot buy trust. We have to earn it. Trust lives on a two-way street. Total dedication to the cause of trust long-term brings its rewards in abundant measure. We cannot live without Trust at the helm of our life.

5.05

THE FIRSTS AND THE
BESTS IN LIFE

The Firsts and the Bests in life can be many. They may not be as many, or the particular ones, as we would want them to be. The good Firsts, the good Bests have a thrill and a glamour all their own. The not-so-good Firsts or the Firsts we hate or we despise are our unwanted experiences. We all hope that the good Firsts and the Bests have been prominent and remain so in our life. Now, all on our own, let us venture onto our individual life scene, complex and intriguing as it may be. Let each one of us explore a very few of our Firsts and a very few of our Bests.

We begin with our first recall. From babyhood to adulthood we are kissed and hugged many times by friends and acquaintances, and maybe as often as or maybe not as often as we in our turn kiss, embrace and hug our parents, our family and our friends, and our dear ones. Nearly all these kisses are a manifestation of affection and of friendship, but in this there are some kisses that are but a formality. Many of these kisses continue as the years go by, and in all this there emerges early on or late in life, the First Kiss of the two people who have begun a love relationship packed with wonder, packed with glory, packed with the art of love at its finest. There is an intuitive sense of wanting each other, making each other our very own. We reach the mountain top on the crescendo for both. We begin to communicate understanding and commitment. A romantic allurement is on the scene for both. We see a sweeping view of our world, and before long we lean forward and bend for a kiss. We have dreams. We have goals. When all is said and done, this particular First Kiss remains forever etched in our memory.

First Love makes its entry. We meet a person of the opposite sex. This is not the first person we have met, but it is a person who stirs within us, within the innermost enclave in us a sensation that is unparalleled. The sensation is deep; it is all-encompassing. It lights a spark. Immediate or not, the closeness and the affectionate feeling for and of this individual grows. If it is mutual and there is reciprocity, a new life, a new adventure begins for both. It is your First Love. If only you have the depth of the feeling, and the other side does not, and the response is only for a short time, or is unfulfilling in a particular manner for either side, our first love to be born may not be our true first love. The episode can be damaging, it can be a little destructive for us, it can take its place in our life story, hopefully without hurt to either side. On the other hand, our first love that is on firm ground can be our triumph. We treasure our loved one. We will soon huddle for warmth. The first love for both can be a fulfilling, exciting adventure, unrivalled and unparalleled. We only live once, and we want to live it near perfect.

Let us move on. We begin with our First Look at Somebody Special, who is now somebody we value, we prize. We see and we meet. We associate with hundreds of people, and at some stage in our life, early on or late or somewhere in between, we take our first look at somebody special. We stand back. We stand in admiration of the person. The person raises our consciousness. All this makes us honor the person. We see in the person so much that is powerful in one or more spheres of life. There is power that comes from certain attributes that glow forth. There is morality, character, personality, capability and graciousness, so dominant, so unrivalled, so appealing to us. This person may even touch off an ambition in us. We discern in this person so much that is precious. All this captures, and then takes over our attention. We remain in admiration of this Somebody Special.

We come to our Best Friend. We may have many friends at different stages in life. Some become good friends. Friendship is not necessarily instant. It begins with a sense of compatibility. From within this group of people emerges our best friend. This is a friend with whom we have some common interests, with whom we have established and maintained a rapport, with whom we have developed and cultivated mutual respect. We are friends who listen attentively to each other and who help each other when the need arises. The bond of friendship is strong and enduring. Both sides give much to the other, without counting the cost. We do not tend to waver on matters affecting our friendship or on the needs of each other. We pray we may all be blessed with our Best Friend.

We move on to our next recall. This can be our Best Success, which thus far has been real. On our horizon, it is visible in all its grandeur. We have prepared for it. We have worked for it. We have invested time, resources and effort in it. We have experienced sweat and tears. Our resourcefulness has been tested. Our creativity has been at work. We

SEARCH FOR LIFE'S GLORY, SENSE LIFE'S PAIN

have been to the fountain of youth. We have made our abode at the fountain. Success is not always from the book. We have had to show initiative, enterprise and constancy that we prize as our own. We either meet the challenges in our path, or we could lie down and perish. Thank God, we have not surrendered. We have persevered. We have had our frustrations. We have overcome them. We greet our best success. We are thankful. We are overwhelmed. It is the advent of our development of a self-image that we take pride in. We know that in most areas we have to take the limits off our life. We begin to appreciate the self-fulfillment of our many goals as they take place. This Best Success brings us our great moments of Life's triumphs.

We are growing up as young women and young men. We have seen our family members and people around us work, earn their keep and more, and justly attain success. We learn from them and about them, about their competence and about their work capability. We develop a desire to get our First Job and take pride to earn our first paycheck, small and inconsequential as the job may be, small as the paycheck may be. The thrill is unforgettable. While on this first job, we might leave soon to make the selective choice of decision alternatives for what we would like to be workwise, in what occupation we would like to make our work career. Our First Job remains our First.

Our Graduation Days are always among the Best Days in our life. The days bring happiness. The days bring a sense of triumph. The days are in school. The days are in college. We feel a strong sense of achievement. Many around us have earned our gratitude. All through our school and our college days, our dear mother, our dear father, all in the family have motivated us, encouraged us and supported us in many ways.

Our teachers, our professors, our counsellors have been the backbone of so much that we have learned, so much that we have gained, even when our performance, our attitude, our concentration may have wavered, may have needed propping up, may have needed boosting up, may have had to be grounded in moral and ethical principles. Both groups of people — family and educators — have made a super contribution to our life and to our future. On the groundwork that has been laid and developed, it is now up to us to proceed to search for the glory of life, and to find it at different stages of our life and in different areas of involvement.

Hopefully, there are many more Firsts and many more Bests in our life. All we have done here is recall a few, a very few. We have just entered in, and are walking down the garden path of the Firsts and the Bests in our Life. Let each of us continue on this journey, and relive from time to time the glory of our life, the specials in our life.

PERCEPTIONS OF LIFE

NEW BEGINNINGS

We sit still and ponder. Life moves on at a hastened pace, or at a more regulated pace. Each of us is at a different stage on life's horizons. We pause in our thinking. We go deeper into our concentration on life. We suddenly become aware that a new dawn is in the offing. A New Beginning is to be made. We accept that it is never too late to make a new beginning in many sectors of life's activity, in most phases of life's cycle. A new beginning can be the fore-runner of yet another, and another accomplishment in life.

A new beginning can be for a better life. Sometimes we may feel we cannot afford to make a new beginning because of the problem we face or we foresee, or because of the effort involved. But in many instances we cannot afford not to make a new beginning, even when there is the magnitude of the task ahead and the fear of possible disappointment and failure.

We may be 18, we may be 30, we may be 60 and beyond, and regardless of our age, some of us do not become hesitant about making a new beginning. In certain sectors of activity, age can be a factor. In other cases, age can be inconsequential. Nothing should deter us from searching out for a new beginning. We must become motivated to achieve our full potential and more. We must remove, we must banish the restraints placed on us intentionally and unintentionally by ourselves or by others.

It is but human to be intimidated by likely problems. At times we will deny the problem's existence, even when it is embedded in the scene. We are not to be dwarfed or humbled by our earlier experiences, however deadly they may have been. We are not to be trapped between need and want.

Reality should not intimidate us. On the contrary, once we have assessed the situation, we should muster the strength and the conviction to make a new beginning. We have to select our destiny, wherever and whenever we can. We have to condition ourselves to be content in the direction we have set ourselves. We must persevere to the goal. An imposed, productive discipline enters and grows in our life.

We are not to create expectations too soon. In our thinking, we are not to ascend unrealistically to Cloud Nine. Unless we make proper and informed judgements, we may find ourselves lodged in the depths of the well. When setbacks confound us, it is incumbent on us to rethink, retool and try again. Sometimes, the old thinking may and can ring hollow, and it may be out of line with today's needs. Sometimes, it has all the wisdom of maturity and of opportunity. Remember failure can be an orphan.

Once we have made a new beginning and we have withstood the many challenges that come our way, we are better equipped to make another new beginning, and another new beginning in the multiple challenges on life's adventure. Success is then more often astride in our path. One more success with a new beginning is better than no success from the fear of making a new beginning.

We must be committed to change things, when change can

be rewarding. We will spend every day of our life working on change, and change for the better. We learn that life is a struggle, personally and interpersonally. Without a new beginning, much of the fullness in the magnificence of life is never created. Life can remain barren, and we should see that it does not. We should make as many new beginnings as we need to, as we want to. Our intuitive excellence and our power must surface, and remain prevalent. Life can be more fulfilling, more triumphant with the success of each New Beginning. Celebrate life in all its glory.

LANDSCAPES OF LIFE

For each one of us, all in life begins with the day of birth. For many of us the pattern is: the first four years, early school days, teenage years, the Twenties, Midlife or another label we might prefer for the latter. Life could then proceed to the Fifties, the Seventies, the Post-Seventy years. How full of wonder and opportunity our God has made the mystery of life for us all! At all stages, Life has been as great as a mountain of opportunity laid before us. Life's future beginning with today is complex and unrevealing, but hopefully, rewarding.

Our small, helpless beginnings become our introduction to the enigmatics of life. In our early years every need, every desire that others determine for us is ministered to. In these years, we do not participate in this determination, except in strange babyways in which we make or do not make known our feelings, or we tend to express or not express ourselves. Our own needs may go unheeded because we cannot conceive them, because we are not understood and because we cannot communicate directly. In this babyhood, we are given more attention, more care, more tenderness than we will ever receive. The unacknowledged joy of babyhood is, in a hidden sense, exhilarating, and largely held within ourselves.

Soon the process of growing begins accelerating. It moves on. For us this development will go on until we bid farewell to the world, or until we call a halt to our growing up at any life-stage. However, the later program in life will be so different from babyhood. We will individually participate exclusively in life or we will do so to a large extent.

In babyhood, little by little we show recognition of those around us. We are fed, we are clothed, we are bathed. We are held, cuddled and fondled. We are carried around or we are escorted around. We display glimpses of our affection, and of our liking for those around us and for things we see or little by little we talk about. We relish all this. We begin to learn to share the mutual love that has begun in us, and we want to give love to others.

School life is our first challenge. It is the beginning of an adventure in learning, in education and in being trained. These are the early days of character building. We take our first steps towards establishing our identity — who we are, what we are, who and what we want to be, and what plans and methods we will adopt to create our personality, to attain our identity, and to make that identity prevail. Some of us board the fast track, and work to perform continuously at a level that will result in achievement and in success. Beams of sunshine brighten our lives.

As we approach the teenage years, we often search openly or discreetly for role models. In several aspects of life, our parents can be among our best models. We are nourished by our parents' teaching. In the formative years, the weak among us yield to peer pressure. We are torn between the ideal in life as defined by the prevailing elite in society and our own formulated ideas. The hope is that these two standards will be identical, or be as close together as possible.

As we grow in childhood, we begin to observe people and things. We begin to recognize people and things. We see people who give to others of their being, of their talent and of their time. We learn to acknowledge some likes and dislikes. We learn to remedy the dislikes.

The late Teens and the Twenties take us through our training for an occupation, for a profession. We learn to discipline ourselves as we work around those who have been in the mainstream of activity and those who like ourselves are new entrants in this aspect of life. We get educated to boost our character and our personality. Power of all dimensions is released within us. We search for and in many cases accomplish our goals and our objectives. Everyday we prepare for the challenges of life to come. We grow more mature, more accomplished.

Around us, we see a people that is occupied with attention to different aspects of society. We see time devoted to a whole range of activities. We see the juggle of families, the burdens and the responsibilities. In our journey in life, we make happy discoveries, some great and some less encouraging. We learn that prominence can be exhilarating initially, and that it has a regulated place on the life scene. We sit back, we deliberate and we evaluate. We strive for adjustments and for changes in our own life. We do not always accept what is portrayed before us. We see a sullen atmosphere. We see a dignified atmosphere. Some of us live in the belief that our destiny is spelled out for us, but that we do not know the specifics of it all. We sigh, we shout, we scream. We laugh, we rejoice.

We reach the stage at what can be described as Middlelife. We are established in life; we are, hopefully, moving progressively on life's path. We are in the midst of success and accomplishment, or we are immersed in the less favorable in life, or we find ourselves in turmoil. We must build on all the good we have attained, and we must correct the less promising. We must remember that there are no easy solutions. The power within us can be great, it can be monumental, if we demonstrate the control we exercise. We must not let time race by. We must not sit back. We must not resign ourselves to the unrelenting signs of defeat that appear on life's scene. We must develop our traits and our talents, however much the perseverance costs us in life's resources. We might have to live under a new agenda, a new structure, and best of all a new confidence in ourselves.

Before we reach Middlelife, preferably in the late Twenties, we must devote time and effort to planning for the middlelife stage of our life and for later in life. We must recognize that nobody, nobody other than we ourselves will take care of me and you. Government will not be, and cannot be expected to be there in the specifics we want them to. In the society of the early twenty-first century and beyond, we cannot be guaranteed that the work pension benefits will be life's bonus on which we will place our future dependence. In the competitive world of the next century, pension plans may not be around us in the form they are today and have been for the past two generations. Availability of government pensions and employer pension plans to meet our needs may not always be the basic or the additional resources at our command. If we work on our goals, we can take care of our finances, beginning the process as early in life as we can. We have to undertake financial planning and estate planning on our own, and with the help of others knowledgeable in the fields. We must remain dedicated to this challenge. In this, through our own research, we must create and develop our knowledge base. There is a wealth of information-base and more around us, and in order to build our castle we can seek help from friends and in some areas we can receive professional assistance. The financial and estate worlds are complex, and are ever-changing, more so now and in the future than in earlier years. We should be alert to change in the intriguing realm of government policies and regulations and the challenging market in money, particularly the more-than-ever emerging global scene. We will deservedly pat ourselves on the back when we succeed in these areas. We must make our personal and family estate and our finance a continuous field of interest in our lives, bringing all our family into this orbit of the present and the future. The global scene as it affects each one of us individually is growing in complexity, and we can and we must build our confidence and our competence.

Soon more of the Fifties will be with us. Some will resign themselves to being on the edge of retirement from an active life. They feel inclined to take a back seat in life. They become less enterprising. They live in the conviction that they are more into relegating themselves to doing little or doing nothing new or out of the routine, the ordinary. They will either live the pattern of the past, or even recede from the heights of the past. There are others in the Fifties, who, apart from their lifelong professions and occupations, will enter into new enterprises, even seek adventure in a new, more rewarding lifestyle. They will achieve. In the process, they will become an excellent demonstration of how humanity should live even as they enter the second half of their very own century. We stand in admiration of these people, people who will age gracefully.

In the Fifties, or before or after, many see in their own life their new family generation of grandchildren on the scene. A rewarding blend of happiness enters their life. They give a striking example of the story that it is not your age, but your attitude to life and life's happenings that determine whether you are old, whether you act old and whether you have outlived the good in life. The saying is that some people begin and continue aging. They start getting old in their young thirties, their young forties and their young fifties. Some people live young and enterprising in their sixties and in their seventies and beyond. The latter group still think young, and they act gracefully young. They function with a maturity that is commendable. They are to be applauded.

As we move into the seventies, our approach to life can and in many cases does change, a change that has a distinct bearing on the quality of our life. Do we live our life, or do we exist from day to day? We must do all we can to live in the best way we can, not merely to be in the barrenness and the emptiness of life. As we grow, we must stay with special emphasis on the best elements in life. We may have some or many restrictions placed on us by our health, our resources, our human concerns. Despite all this, let us do all we can to live our life to the fullness of our capability and the range of our competence.

One major concern, or maybe more than one major concern, prevails in the seventies and in the post-seventy years. One is health and the other is wealth, the latter even in a modest, unassuming way. If we have lived a good, productive life and have been blessed, we approach in a positive sense the adventure of the seventies and later, and live happy and content. If we have deficiencies in health and in financial condition, we can carry new burdens into these seventies and beyond. Some of these emanate from neglect and lack of proper planning and failures of execution of plans in earlier times.

With proper advice and guidance, we may be able to correct some or all of these problems at this late stage in life, if we bring ourselves around the more mature thinkers and performers. As we scan life's scenario, we must accept as a fact of life that we may have choices, or sadly, we resign ourselves to the probability that we may have none.

What happens next? Today, we see life moving faster and at an increasing pace now than it was in the 1960s and the 1970s. The landscape for all can be richer, it can be greener. It is also fraught with a wider range of difficulties and complexities. The landscape can and will undergo change. The questions posed for us are: Can we change from the present to the way we want life to be? Can we regulate some of life's pace to conform to our goals? Laxity in not wanting to better oneself is wrong. Let us devote some attention to the transient nature of life. Let us brace ourselves to move on. Let us not stay buried in the sands of time.

Many of the features we have related are the positive aspects in the landscapes of life. There can be many negatives or near-negatives with some of them self-inflicted with different causes, different reasons. Do not live in the mounting regret that we could have done better. If we have waited too long, the remedies may no longer be within our field of action. We may never have had choices, but we might have been able to seek alternatives. Sit back for a moment. Let us recall the good and the great things we have done, and this mode can better our chances to be in green pastures in the coming ages of our life.

If we find ourselves on a positive path in life, and we confirm this when we view the landscape from the hilltop or on our climb up, we do well to pause briefly and to pat ourselves on the back. We deserve this self-compliment. We are on the proper journey. Our life has been fulfilling in many ways, and, if it has not, it is never too late to make amends in some areas and to journey on to the richness of the rainbow in the breaking sunshine in the landscape of our lives. We can always make our landscapes of life better and richer than they are today. Let us resolve to do this.

DREAM AND DREAM, AGAIN AND AGAIN

Time has left its footprints. Do not embitter the present by living in some of the frustrations of the past. Do not be shuttered in or be shrouded by failure and disappointment. Never despair, for despair invites defeat. We are in need, not because we do not possess the good of life in any of its many forms, but because we choose to live our lives without a dream. In the darkest days when we are hurt, scarred and humbled, when we have sunk into the depths, when our fondest dreams have been crushed, dream and dream, again and again.

Keep our hearts young, and our dreams will stay with us. Achievement is fueled by dreams. We may falter, we may sometimes seem to fail. Do not quit or succumb into self-pity. Get ourselves back into contention. March on. Dream on, undaunted. Learn to hope anew, brace up, and we will not be denied the good in life. Every hindrance may be yet another challenge. We can and we will conquer. Keep in our own world our dream of changing for the better.

Life's triumphs, small and big, are bought with human toil and tears and sweat. Success comes after effort is stripped of its doubts. Time will bring joy, time will bring faith, such as nothing can mar or destroy. At no time should we take for granted our confidence, our fame and our reputation, however big or small any of these are. We must keep working at preserving them, fostering them to grow even more.

Every day is precious. Life may take strange twists and turns. Keep the faith. At times, it may seem that we trudge too often uphill and seemingly all alone. Plod on, though we feel faint, or find ourselves stumbling, worn and weary with a heavy load. Tomorrow's triumphs are born of our dreams of today.

Live surrounded by God and work with him to share or to carry the burden. We follow the path of our visions beyond, and let God lead. He sees our tears, our torments. He knows our anguish, our trials, our crosses. He knows the complexities of our task. Strive on in the conviction that we lean upon a strength beyond our own.

The goals in life are nearer than we think. With God, our heart will be mysteriously disburdened. We need God's helping hand, which may come through the presence of a friend. At times, we need a strength beyond our own. We need a power beyond our own. Remember we are never alone. Our strength begins with our God. God will make us equal to our task.

As the day is nearing its end and the night closes in, pause for a few extra moments. We can be weary, whether we have experienced triumph or failure. We can have the life we want, if we do all that is required to attain this. Let thankfulness swell in our hearts, for God will give us another day, and another and another, in order to create success and to transform failure into a new triumph. Rest on his promise, knowing he will not fail those who with him have dared to achieve, to dream and to dream, again and again. Today's dreams can become tomorrow's reality if we strive to make them so. We know we cannot let ourselves down. We must carry our ideas and our plans to fruition. So dream, dream again and again, even dream forever.

THE DANCE OF LIFE

One of the most complex issues we face is life itself. Is anyone's life simple, or can it become simple? No, it is not, and it cannot become simple. It cannot be made simple. The complexities of life, the intricacies of life vary from one person to another. Life can be propelled to achievement and to greatness by happenings, and, on the opposite side, life can be marred and made gloomy by unwanted events. At times, we can have some control of our lives, while at other times we cannot and do not, however much we may want to, however much we may try to. Even after setbacks, we must continue in our quest to gain control and direction in our life.

What does life conjure up in our mind? We all have only one life to live. For us, this life is not a practice night or a dress rehearsal for the real life. Everyday, every moment, this is the real life. It is our one lifelong stage performance spread over our lifetime measured in hours, days and years. The stage is set and reset for us many times. With no original script at birth, no practice and no rehearsal, we have therefore to live this one life in frequently changing stage scenes as best we can, writing or rewriting some of the developed script or some of the developing script whenever we can.

In life a smorgasbord is laid before us. At times much or all of the smorgasbord is spread out before us, and at other times there is more of life's complexity, its beauty, richness and grandeur yet to come. All of us have something special to offer, something precious to give to ourselves and to those around. At the smorgasbord of life, we sample, we taste, we feast. At certain times we can be selective, but at times the choice to make is not entirely ours, not largely ours.

Life is a dance. On some of life's stages we dance alone. At other times, we dance with partners who may be our spouse, our children, our parents, our family, our friends, our work associates. We do not want to dance with strangers or with the unknown. We dance in today's current life scenario. We may dance in the unborn happenings of tomorrow and beyond. Some of us may be pointed to and search for personal finery in particular phases of the dance of life. We can attain success, we can achieve if we try and find out how to discover success, and then work at it.

We can agonize and languish in life searching for a guide, a mentor, a shepherd, a sponsor, who may be more than one person. We could be blessed with an individual with all these virtuous roles merged into one being, or this person could be us personally. In the search, however long this may be, we may not be able to find outside ourselves any of these special people or even some of them. We may have to be on our own, and we can be. In the challenges of everyday living, we can then seek, if we need to, the alternative of a support group to cheer us on.

In the dance of life, the dance music, the dance tune change often. We come face to face with difficult issues, with diverse and complex choices. We grapple with them. We set our priorities. Ignorance may breed fear. Life may be perplexing, failure may stare us in the face, but we must not surrender. We have to learn to live by our wits, by the courage of our convictions, by our intuition, by our ingenuity. We must depend on our instincts, our values. We cannot be impulsive in our behavior. Success can be ours through the search for knowledge and skill. All this becomes part of the dance of our life, to the degree we want it to become.

We cannot, and we would not want to walk away from the dance of life. The grace and the majesty of the dance can be irresistible. The only enemy of any description for us is not the society we live in, but we ourselves, not wanting to achieve or being too timid to accept the challenges of life. We can be our enemy. We can grow or we can remain unprepared and ill-equipped. But we must resolve not to be induced away from the grandeur of the dance of life.

God has a plan and a dream for each of us, each plan and each dream uniquely formulated for our individuality, for our personality, and for who we, and for who we alone, are. There might be the daily frenetic activity. Every day we must have the predilection to separate and set our priorities in the challenges which confront us. It has been said that in the dance of life, we can and we do stumble over pebbles before we can come to the mountain climb.

We all have dreams. We all set goals in different areas, in different dimensions. We can formulate a defined time schedule which in life's turmoil may be and can be fractured, a little too frequently sometimes. As we proceed, we pause to reassess. We reassemble. This is the time when, on the path to success, we tend to take some comfort in small gains, followed by gains of some size for us. Self-esteem becomes important in our life. We grapple with a variety of issues, some self-ignited, some not. We empower ourselves. We display a winning attitude. We create opportunities where none existed, and did not remotely seem to exist. You and I can offer our life and the life of others all that is uniquely ours.

Remember, we were brought to the dance floor at birth. As time went on, we were made to become and on our own became more and more aware and conscious of the music of life. We experience the beauty of life, and also the less desirable rhythm of life. We make our decisions to participate in certain pieces of music in the dance of life. Remember, dance in life we must. We can dance amidst joy and happiness. You and I can work to make the world dance happily with us. Let us do this.

_____

6.05

Invest in Life

All of us invest in life. We must. Our creator wants us to do that. We draw on the bank we are building within our innermost self. In our lives we invest resolve, resources, time, energy and commitment. Some do this with clearly defined objectives and with purposeful determination. We do this because we must each live a productive life in every sense of the word, in every activity of this productive life.

Some do their investment in life unplanned and with no set goal in mind. Before we draw on the bank, we must search for our positive opportunities. We investigate personal growth prospects. For all the best we seek in life, we have to invest in life. But, as we know from life's experiences, some of what we and our fellow beings invest in life may not all be positive or productive to ourselves and to society at large. Sadly, some of us invest in doing little or nothing, in doing wrong, in doing evil. In this writing, we will dwell in a small way on this disappointing aspect of society.

We will now portray the positives. Many of us invest in learning, and we grow in knowledge. This knowledge enables us to acquire and to develop skills. In this plan of ours, we advance skillwise. We advance intellectually, economically and financially. We grow in stature. Our careers progress on or are propelled to higher levels. We attain success. We even triumph. The world around us gives us recognition. Our achievements can be credited to more than one facet — our inborn capability, our ability at learning and being trained, our ability to be ardently competitive, our talent to achieve and to win acclaim in the midst of many others who have also invested in life and have grown in learning and in knowledge.

Some of us invest in lifestyles, striving to outdo and to outpace others, or at the very least to be better than others, or to be not less than on a low par. In this our success is derived largely from self-approbation and from the superior stature to preferably be among the elite and the dominant company in society that we feel we should seek. Our investment in this field can gain us focus in society, and sometimes a feeling of being among the exclusive. We want to be in the societal hierarchy. When we do this, we reckon we have attained the ultimate, dubious as that may appear to be to some.

A select group invest in a certain section of virtuous living. We sense the misery of fellow beings in the world around us, and we will do all we can to contribute to the recovery of their well-being. We find ourselves in a position to release some energy we do not directly require to keep. We are convinced that for others much needs to be done. We are pledged to devote whatever resources we can to the cause. As we proceed we can get so immersed in the cause. In the ultimate our great reward is to recognize some alleviation of the problem, even if our personal effort makes only a small dent. We proudly and justly feel we have helped to accomplish.

For a few of us, investment in life takes the form in dedicating much of our life or a part of our life in giving gratuitous service pro bono to our fellow beings. This group is to be saluted for their dedication, their perseverance and for the manner in which they will face and often overcome obstacles in their path.

Some among us invest in serving their fellow citizens in the halls of government at all levels and in the corridors of community and national service. Among these are some who are super achievers and a credit to their citizenry.

We give recognition to the ministries of religion in both sexes who invest in life by their lifelong dedication of service to their flock. They are to be revered, honored and admired. Many in certain denominations are devoted to their cause and to their people, and operate within their community for laudable objectives. They bring credit to their vocation in life.

Some of us invest in fashionable dress and fashionable living. We always want to be trendy, or we aim to be the percussor of trends yet to come into society. We rejoice in this investment. It fulfils our dreams and our objectives, limited as they may be. We feed on our feelings of self-acclamation. If this particular investment trend is not controlled, it can become self-defeating.

Then we have those who invest in life attempting to gain some concentration on how to beat the system. They have difficulty in acquiring a good knowledge of the system and how to make it work for them. So they run counter to the system, and sometimes bring their evil mind sectors into play. This category of individuals embraces those who indulge in crime of all dimensions. Guile, greed, evil and an overriding disregard of others dominate their thinking and their actions. They do so in the expectation that this investment can be the forerunner of a dubious sense of achievement. When the worst overtakes those who experience any of this investment in life, the feeling of a search for vengeance overpowers their outlook.

Some of us invest in life with our sights set on the time in our lives when we will move into retirement from an active work life. This is a praiseworthy long-term investment to be encouraged in all of us. We must deliberate on alternatives. We must evaluate opportunities. We must consider acquiring new skills, new interests and new goals. There is much that we can accomplish in our vision of the future.

We must recognize that at times it is not enough to invest in extending life, merely for life to be without quality, for it to be achievementless and much less than happy. In these situations, life's extension can prove hurtful. To the very end, life has to be made worth living. Life must have quality in the way that suits each one of us best. After a certain stage in our life, we must not merely exist, and we mean just exist. We must do all we can to make life meaningful and purposeful with a sense of happiness. Old age is a stage which can vary with all individuals. Some can be old at 50, others not before they are 60, 70, 80 or beyond. Again, we need not just be without goals, small as they may be. We need not just move along without purpose. Regardless of age, we can move into new areas of achievement and satisfaction. We need a quality in life, defined in terms best applicable to our past, and each day perhaps in new and not over-ambitious horizons.

Regrettably, there are those who invest in life by sitting back and doing little or nothing. They just sit back, grin and groan. They may be hostile to the world. They see others grow and prosper in all that matters in life, the good they themselves lack. Pathetically, their investment in life can be described as doing nothing. They become a futile commentary on an investment in life that cannot only not pay any returns or grow in value, but an investment that is doomed to abysmal failure even before it starts. They are people who could have invested profitably in life, even to a minor extent at the start, but they do not do so. They are people who have to be encouraged, motivated and propelled, but they are not receptive enough to advice and to efforts for help. If they do not want to join the fight for the better things in life, they have to be energized and hurled into the inner ring of the gainful and rewarding investment avenues of life.

In all of our investment in life, some of us succeed, some fail. Some succeed beyond their expectation, some fall into an abyss. Any thought of failure in our good investments in life should not deter us from pursuing our goals. Prospect of failure should rather make us assess and reassess all aspects of the situation before we proceed to invest in life or decide not to make the investment. We must remember that when we venture into a new field or extend our frontiers, we will not be frightened if we are properly prepared, because every achiever was once a starter. Failing to plan can lead us into planning to fail.

Investment in life can in some cases bring us hurt and disappointments. It can weaken us. It can make us dispirited and prone to surrender. It is at this time that we recognize that winning is not all-encompassing. At the same time, defeat has nothing to suggest we give failure or adversity any prolonged or damaging prevalence in our thinking, as this affects our future.

Investing in life should be in fields which are in conformity with our character, our personality, our abilities, our motivation and our aspirations. Achievement must flow from within ourselves. We have to take total command of ourselves. We have to exhibit total confidence in ourselves. We have to develop a glamour and a charisma all our own. On every occasion, we should give to the world the best version of ourselves. We must make the expression of ourselves our dream. We should check our goals and our directions. The only regret we may have is that we did not do what we could have done at the time it could have been done. But this regret should not remain on the scene with us.

Our ambition should be to make every day a masterpiece or a near masterpiece of life to the maximum extent that we can, with a definition of the masterpiece uniquely appropriate to the best in us. It is said that we should be judged for what we can do, not for what we cannot. For all involved, invest in life with a good, compounding return on the investment, depositing back in the end in the bank of life much more than we ever withdrew from it. If we succeed in this goal, we will have built our wealth and our investment in life in the greatness of our own day by day living.

OUR LIFE CAN REACH THE HILLTOP

For many of us, life can be viewed from a different cliff on the hilltop every day, and, maybe, several times during the same day. At times this viewing can be encouraging, fulfilling and beneficial; at times it can be disappointing, it can be disheartening, it can be devastating.

Much depends not only on the scene before us, but on the viewer. That person's psychology, perspective, motivation, life's experiences and ambitions and confidence in oneself can have a direct effect on what we see. For many of us, these six elements create the mode, the mood, the attitude. They lend direction to action or inaction. They sew the seeds of growth and happiness, or they let the weeds thrive with life not being tended.

If the direction is negative, there rapidly develops an atmosphere of moroseness, hopelessness, a sense of desperation and a resignation to helplessness. It can be worse. It can lead one to resigning oneself to abandonment, to fate which is described as "lying down and dying", or worse still propelling one to unbecoming and unsocial behavior, harming oneself and those around us. None of this must happen in any significant way, in any irreparable way, and, least harmful of all, in any way whatever.

Even when the direction is negative, it behooves those driven to despair and the most despondent among us to search for the distant cloud with the proverbial silver lining. Tunnel vision must be replaced by full dimension vision.

No situation is hopeless, no situation is beyond repair. We must not confess to hostility. We can learn to accept criticism without resentment. If we cannot handle the not-so-good, the not-so-promising, then we need counsel, best of all counsel from a trusted and a knowledgeable friend. The light at the end of the tunnel should never die out. Hope is transcendent even in the midst of adversity.

Our vision and our vocation can appear dimmed. They can be dreary. They can be bright. They can project the unexpected. We have to control conflicting demands. We have to learn to manage and to be selective of life's priorities. Negativism, rage, abandonment of hope, and humiliation that we feel must be, and can be brushed aside.

The power of our intellect, however small, however limited should be given all the opportunity to surface and to grow. We must set, and, maybe, reset out goals and our objectives. In terms of our own personal resources and abilities, we should seek what is attainable. We should not berate ourselves. We should not seek what is beyond us. Life does not promise us immediate rewards. As we journey along, we get the sense of the coming triumph. Before long, we will see progress and achievement and success. Confidence in ourselves will build. We will ascend to the hilltop and see a great view. Our ambitions, our desires will grow in this new environment.

Life does not promise us immediate rewards. Once we have

been to the bright, promising hilltop, we will want to proudly return there again and again. Each visit gives us the abundance of life in the sense of triumph as we journey along. We have built and are continuing to build our strengths, our forte to reach the hilltop, and our rewards will be awaiting us when we have deservedly earned them.

———————————————

6.07

THE DREAM AND
THE GLORY

I have had so many hopes, so many expectations, so many dreams, and during all this time many a moon has shone in its brilliance. I have had small dreams, and I have had big dreams. I have built little boats and I have built grandiose castles. In my small dreams, in my attainable dreams, I have lived in hope, and I have been rewarded. I paddled in the water, watching the ducks gracefully glide by. I saw dreams realized. Then, I had my wild dreams. I rejoiced in the success of some of these. For others in my wild array, for my wildest dreams, there seemed to be but a slim chance of success, of achievement, of reward. Nevertheless, I never surrendered. I nurtured within myself the belief that hope was eternal. In this, too, I earned some success, less than the greatest it could have been.

Even when I scaled down my hopes and my dreams in my more ambitious projects, recognition of the chances of realization continued to be slim or nonexistent, and at times receding. This did not deter me from plodding on.

I persevered in my hopes and in my dreams, trusting in the goodness and the magnanimity of my Creator, and in every way taking comfort in the support from those who cared for me. These were my friends. I confided in a precious few, and these few were always a tower of strength. They made me feel that even in the darkest of the dark hours, there are only sixty minutes.

Time went by. Years started to take their toll. The lack of success began to concern me, to bear down on me. I felt discouraged, disappointed and frustrated, and the realism of my humanity and its constraints came to the fore. In the midst of this, I looked for and I received support and encouragement never to give up. I learned that abject surrender had no role in my life.

Then one fine day, without any special heralding, there was a turn of events. I sat back. I saw hope dawn, and gradually glow on the horizon. Events began to take shape. Pieces of the mosaic, complex as the mosaic was, emerged to fall into place. I pinched myself to assure myself that this was real. I had to tread with caution. I had to remain on my guard for fear of making a wrong, and, maybe, a fatalistic move. I recognized that I had a major and a crucial part to play in the reality that the dream had brought about. If I was to see the glory of the dream, all the best that was in me would be brought to the fore.

I had to take time to compose my thoughts, and to plan my strategy and my actions. Self-centeredness could take me into isolation. As a first step, I lay down and let my dream chart its course. The sea could be stormy; the sea could be calm. In my life thus far, a long period of deliberation and worldly experience had wizened me, and made me know that I had the skill to work hard and to sail to success. The glory of this, my greatest dream thus far, was magnificent. I had an obligation to myself to give of my best. Negative thoughts could lead to confrontation. I acknowledged that I owed much to the resolve nurtured within me.

I was standing at the point of capturing my dream, and to proceeding to live its glory. In the course of my life I knew that the reality was that I would have to make some sacrifices, needless to say, maybe even major sacrifices. I knew that at time the pain would burn deep and fierce. I accepted the possibility of all this. I stood back. I cried out with joy. I laughed. I revelled in all that lay before me. I warned myself to watch every step, major and minor. Every new day brought a challenge and ecstasy. I was beginning to live the first strands of the glory of my dream. I was on the edge of discovering the strength and the conviction within me. I knew that I had to cultivate the mindset of an achiever.

Those who know me can call me a dreamer. Maybe in the eyes of most of them I am. I know that I recognize I am. I pray I will always be. I know that you, too, can be a dreamer, a dreamer in many ways. You and I should have the passion that makes for the life of a dreamer. I pray that you and I will learn all about the dream of life and the magnificence of the glory of life. Let us all be in the wave and in the tide of the dream that flows for all of us to the glory in our own life. Let us all learn that when we win, we must win in a spirit of humility, and when we lose, we must lose with dignity. This is indeed a compelling aspect of the glory in life.

LIFE'S TANGLES
AND WRANGLES

7.01

LIFE CAN BE INTRIGUING

L ife is anything but plain and simple. It has many elements, many ingredients. Many a time it is difficult to understand the patterns within our own life, to understand their purpose. We humans make life more perplexing, more intriguing, every day of our life. We simplify issues, we complicate issues. We ignore issues. It takes purpose, direction and determination from each of us to focus on the complexities of life, many a time so dissimilar for each of us.

In the mysteries of life, there is success, there is happiness. In the same life, there is pain and there is anguish. As we proceed on life's path, we must acknowledge the presence of all these elements, the good, the not-so-good and, at times mournfully, the bad.

Choices have to be made. Some are simple choices, made with effortless ease. Some are more complex, more involved. Much of the day we have to make conscious choices followed, at times, by difficult detail decisions. Some are moral choices. Some are choices involving life's many principles bearing on conduct, values, integrity, decorum and the effect that our selections can have on our family and those around us. In some happenings, there are no choices. Events are thrust upon us. We are confronted by events. We are brought face to face with perplexing issues, many a time issues we would rather banish from our spectrum.

Embedded in our personality is not only character, but a continually growing reputation hopefully of all that is good and noble. Our attitudes, our conduct and our expressions have a role in this. In the range of the most difficult and the less difficult situations, the strength of our character must prevail.

Life abounds in trade-offs. We should examine them, we should investigate them, before we make our choices and before we arrive at our decisions. We should not abandon ourselves to the concept that if we sit back, the inevitable has to happen. We have to do all we can to make everything happen in the way that we would like it to happen, and in the way that is best for us.

In life everything, however small, has a price. Much on life's shelf is on display, but it may not be all within reach. It cannot be secured for little or for nothing. Need and ambition play their part. At times our selection becomes a demonstration of our character. There are times when we are fortunate in what comes to us; at other times we earn the success and the benefits of a good decision. Much of our accomplishment stems from our own minds, and can be the growth of a single decision or a sequence of decisions, or a pattern within our personal development. In life's perplexing situations, particularly when choices to be made are before us, the person of who we are or what propels us dominate the scene.

Everyday of our life, we recognize and acknowledge that life is intriguing. We are faced with challenges of all dimensions. In every difficult and intriguing situation, in every challenge before us, we should cultivate a winning attitude and we should do our very best. We should remain confident that God will be with us to do the rest.

THE AGONY OF LONELINESS

This is me standing all alone. This is not the first time in my life that it dawns on me that I am seemingly all alone. For me there is no one in the immediacy of my being. For me there appears to be little or nothing hopeful, constructive or fulfilling around. All seems lost. I wait. I go on waiting, and waiting. Before long, I resign myself to one conclusion, and that is, I conclude that all may be lost.

Life is uneventful. Life is dreary. Life is disappointing. Frustration abounds. Failure has overtaken me. There is nothing to look forward to. I am bored in being alone. It occurs to me that in my search in life, I may have become self-indulgent and drawn some benefit from being alone. But I did not do so before, and I do not now. Hope is not on the horizon. I am on the downward slide, the slippery slope of helplessness. There are no straws, however few, that I can grasp. I would like to forego the feeling that God is absent, that God does not now exist, and perhaps, in my forlorn state, never did.

Earlier today, I was somewhat positive, but as the day moved on, things have not gone right for me. I am now in the grip of the depths of an abyss. I cannot see the bottom, deep, deep down as it probably is. Total darkness reigns all around me. I do not seem to be able to do anything to halt my accelerating decline, let alone gather strength to stop and turn around from what appears to be an impending fall into the precipice. I feel convinced that I am in dismal, helpless distress, all alone with no one with me.

The thought of being alone comes back, and persists. The agony of my loneliness is eroding into my mental fiber. I am feeling unfocused. I am being devoured. All I do to regain my composure appears not to succeed. These are real everyday issues. I cannot deny that in time I, not uncommon to so many of us, will have to confront the realities of illness, old age and death. These all can be part of life, as something that can happen, and in the case of death will happen to any of us someday. I put these aside. But I am discouraged by these real everyday conflicts. I am on the brink of desperation. I am tempted to sit back and do nothing. I continue to brood over my agonizing loneliness. I am shattered by the experience of rejection. I am progressively being destroyed. Every moment I feel a worsening of my predicament. I experience isolation and alienation. I am vulnerable when I am lonely. I feel that all this preys on me in this situation. I am a person in dire need.

Suddenly, the most crucial moment in the cycle of loneliness arrives. I call a halt. It is a halt to deliberate in another vein. In this pause I recognize rather accidentally that I may be the culprit in being the source, the originator and the perpetuator of my agony.

Yes, I begin to deliberate. I continue pondering. I begin to accept that I have partial responsibility, if not total responsibility for my state of affairs, for each of my situations. I must not become dispirited. I wonder if an attempt and a campaign for the solution to my dilemma can be in my hands. I have to learn to stop feeling sorry for myself. I have to learn to gain, and even regain my dignity and then preserve it.

I give myself a jolt to determine that I am experiencing something real. I sit back. I pause for a few moments and reorient my thought system. I am in for a rude awakening. Once again, even more firmly, it occurs to me that I may be, I could be, I am the author, the founder and perhaps the perpetrator of my loneliness. Unprepared as I am, I may have now hit on the turning point. I reassemble my thinking. Instantly, I sense a new strength surge within me to set aside and even banish from my mind all the negative thoughts in which I have been immersed for so long. I discover a new dimension in sensuality.

In a constructive way, I explore my immediate affairs. I aim to be objective. I have to set boundaries and keep within them. I probe deep. This is a wholly new approach to life for me. One bright ray, and then another and another emerge on the horizon of my mind to replace the darkness and the gloom. A glimmer of hope shines forth. Hopelessness and helplessness are to be shunned by me. I begin to strengthen my resolve to lift myself out of the agony of loneliness. I pledge to relieve myself of the weariness that follows misery. I will not allow the water-soaked tears inching down my cheeks to deter me. I will bring to an end the years embittered by my failures, by my inadequacies.

My situation is under review. I begin the analysis. I do the analysis without self-pity, without remorse, without regret for the past, without blame on others or on circumstances and situations that have been a part of my life. I should not turn my back, as this will only make the situation worse. I accept that some of the past can always be a part of the present and a part of the future, but because of this I do not have to wallow in abject humility.

I determine that I can create interests, where none existed. I can fill the vacuum that was there and was once brimful of the agony of loneliness, close to an overflow. I can use newfound strength to build these interests, one at a time or several in quick succession to be coordinated simultaneously. I see how I can immerse myself in several activities, maybe a little cautiously at first. I must resolve to keep my chin up. I must not stick my neck out.

My battle against loneliness begins to gain strength. I will not allow persistent fears and overwhelming anxiety to deter me. I set myself on the road to a more constructive life, achieving good things and not accepting me being a loser in the agony of loneliness. For me, out of the bleakness of darkness has sprung the gold of spring.

At this stage, I stand convinced of the emerging positives in life. I feel reassured that darkness does not last for ever. No longer will I walk around with scars inside me. My world is what I, and primarily I, make of it. So let me hurry. Time is precious and there is never too much of time at our command. I have just begun the battle to conquer loneliness, and to overcome the agony that lingers and grows on such as me. The night of loneliness has to be dismissed from my mind. My voice and my mind no longer tremble, my eyes are no longer bathed in torture or in tears. Soon, the agony of loneliness will be banished from my life. I do not want to pretend that I just exist. None of us should. I want to be truly alive, to live, and to live a good life, the best I can do. I am confident that I have just sown the seeds of what, in time, can bloom into a good life. I begin today in all the earnestness that I can bring to bear on my life, and succeed I will. All you who are agonizing in loneliness should join me in this deserving quest of our life.

7.03

STUNG AND IN PAIN

Disappointments, heartbreak and pain are the realities of life. At times it is not only what these occurrences do to us that destroys some part of us, but how we face up to them and then cope or not cope with them. It would be one of the happiest aspects of our life if disappointments, heartbreak and pain could be banished forever from our life, or not be on the scene ever in our life. But in the reality of life that cannot be. We must do the next best. We must reduce the impact of all pain on us.

However hard we try, many times in life we are stung and in pain. We cannot banish these trying phases from our life. We cannot miss to encounter them when they occur. We know that these can come unannounced and at times even unforeseen. In some cases we know that the bad can happen. When the bad does come, we in our pattern of living should have ourselves better prepared than we might be. At different stages in our life, we should assess the aspects of probability and possibility. We should equip ourselves as best we can in the emotional and the material facets, so that we are not trapped unprepared when disappointments, heartbreak and pain jolt us. In all this, we should know that emotions need to be acknowledged. Emotions need recognition. Emotions need to be controlled and dealt with. Hurt and self-pity cannot feed us.

We can be stung and in pain in areas and in circumstances which are the outcome of our own failures, or our own neglect, or our own inadequacies, or in situations over which we have no control and which we could not have avoided. All these categories can be equally damaging, and just as fatal. One series can be more trying than the other. We must give recognition to our own imperfections, our own weaknesses and our own deficiencies. It is essential to acknowledge that in life the atmosphere of vulnerability that surrounds us may not vanish, and it could grow on us.

But there are other situations, when we are broken, deprived, used, manipulated and devastated because some-one has seized on our weakness, and we have experienced exposure to evildoers' attacks on us. This is despicable on the part of those out to harm us and destroy us. We find ourselves stung and in pain, but we now have the added burden of evil involvement by others. We feel ourselves rudderless and without an anchor.

In all this, the pain is very debilitating. We cannot remain stung and in pain. We cannot remain paralyzed by our fears. Learn to let go of pain. We seek deliverance. Healing can also come partly from forgiveness, if and when this becomes appropriate. Recovery may take weeks, months and possibly years, but, if we persevere, each day will make us find new strength and added resolve. For some, work and concentration of mind and effort on the fulfilling aspects of life, away from the hurt, can be the only antidotes for pain.

Pain can emerge from many sources. These could include family situations, losing employment, not receiving recognition or promotion in our occupation, losing favor, a diminishing of prestige and stature, losing a friend, not achieving what we set out to do, failure with its many different features, any one or more of these. Each of these can be most demeaning. In all this, we can use our feelings of good to rid ourselves of some of the pain. We must learn to cope. Solutions may not be within our total command, but we can be on the search for them, and eventually, we can be astonished by what we achieve. We can once again marvel at our competence, our resilience, and maybe even our brilliance.

Many of us have seen considerable, even monumental pain. There are times when we overfocus on the problem and do not give proper attention to the solution. When we are stung and in pain, anger should not be a part of our life. Anger keeps on gnawing and gnawing at the bones in us and soon reaches the inmost flesh. With every sting and pain a little of us should not die, as is the case with many people around us. We should prepare ourselves, and for a short time do all we can to bring the pain to the forefront and to deal with it. In our pain and agony, we may not be in authority in the individual circumstance, but in all majesty we can be our own woman, our own man. As each day breaks, we should look to our God to be our strength for that day, and when we do this, we will discover that anger and pain can and do remain contained and on the path to cure.

A FRIEND IS DEAD

Death shatters the best of us. It is an emotional disaster. Feelings of pain and sadness surface. Death transforms our moods, our feelings, our deportment, our concerns. We pause in our trek. It is a time for an arousal of deep awareness. Often we are unprepared for the devastating emotionalism which follows. All around it is bleak and incredibly lonely. The aura of invulnerability has deep inroads made into it. We take a brief moment to ponder. At times we feel betrayed.

Grief can be overwhelming. The death of a dear one, be it your loved one or a family member or a confidant or a friend dear to you is a sad, stunning blow. Our friend has gone from us, friends in this world. Our friend has gone across our border to the other world. Death is a painful reminder of times that were and will never again be. Death makes us not just pause; it behooves us to stop and think. We grieve for the love and the friendship we have lost, and at times, we never focused on. In the hour of death, our faith is put to the test. We have to share our feelings and our fears. When tragedy strikes, many of our worldly concerns ascend, grabbing us and fleeing into the clouds around us.

Death makes us consider the meaning of life, the significance of events and happenings, the shortness of life, and the abruptness with which life can be terminated. Death can come with a warning, or it can come unannounced, less suspectingly than a thief in the bleak deep of the night.

Death is a traumatic event. Death is often so sudden that the grieved feel denied the chance to meet and say good-bye and farewell. Death is always seen to be unexpected. We are so unprepared, and life is all over. The grieving must be comforted. Their suffering must be channelled, with proper regard for the grieved.

Religion introduces our thinking to the implications and the seeming contradictions that transcend death. In the crisis of death, God rapidly enters our thoughts. We stand devastated by the loss of a dear one. This is the time when to the grieved we should extend personal and prayerful support. We may not be able to ease the grief in sorrow, but we hope we can bring a feeling of comfort. We share the grief with others, but in doing so we must not stand still on life's path. All those who grieve must go on with life, participating in and experiencing life hopefully as best they can even in the sorrow.

Our Creator calls us to our eternal reward. We humans know what it is to lose one we love so much. For some things in life and about death, the human mind can find no answer. One of these elements of life is death itself. We do not know God's ways or the wisdom of his ways. Nevertheless, his will we must meet every day. We ask God for help and plead with him to work with us to carry the burden. We make an earnest appeal for the grieving not to be beaten down in this hour of need.

We may not be able to ease the grief in this sorrow, but we hope that friends around us can bring us feelings of comfort.

There is no understanding of certain aspects of death. At times, we do not have a fuller understanding of the ways of God. We know that life must go on. Our dear dead can be the life, the spirit and the soul of the family. There will never be answers to the questions on our minds as to the final hour or the final days in this tragedy.

The true measure of our friend was that your friend and my friend was a person full of human wonder. Our friend lived a life of fulfillment. In our innermost feelings, we loved our friend. We admired this person for the joy and the happiness, the friendship and the love the friend brought to life itself and to our relationship, and, from what we know, to the relationship with other fellow beings. We celebrate the life; in this context we do not mourn the death.

We know that we loved our friend so much, but God loved his creation even more. We would have loved to see our friend live on. But it had to be otherwise. Our friend has gone, has gone to be at God's banquet, to be under God's wing. We will not do a prolonged mourning of our loss. We may have had our separate spheres of living and of activity. In death we acknowledge that we may not have seen enough of each other. In death, we sense that we will miss the finest in our friend.

There are times when the dying individual knows that there is no recovery to health. The dying do not ask God for a cure or for healing. We ask for the strength and the grace to understand God's most holy will. Prayer and the promise of prayer bring a message of comfort. It is a thoughtful and consoling way to ease the pain of the afflicted. Time heals. The pain of death is dulled by time. We believe this healing, this containment to be true to some extent, even in a large measure.

None of the considerations, none of the elements associated with death will ever change. Let us take a moment to deliberate about our mortal selves. None among us wants to die; we should only want to live with dignity. But in this sphere of life, we as individuals or collectively are not in command. Amidst all our disillusionment, arrives peace and hope.

Death is an unchangeable reality of life. Grief is real in life. Many of us will continue in our old-time approach to death. We grieve. We grieve. We grieve when one dear to us goes to eternity. This grieving is not wrong, even since we know the dead cannot return to life. Grieving is not to be derided. The underlying question is what can come from intense grieving, from labored grieving which generates pain within ourselves. The dead cannot come back to life. We should not wait for the pain of the loss of a loved one to ease with time to a dull ache, and then to disappear. We need to view death in a different perspective.

Think out grief. Work out grief. Do not let grief take possession of you. Numbness and frustration must not take command of you. Do not hold grief within you for any extended length of time, however short it may seem to you. Learn to give focus to the life around you, for life is to proceed each day without our dear friend. The crisis in its loneliness becomes personal, and we have to manage it without significant hurt to ourselves.

In recent years we have seen a remarkable change in some people's approach to the death of a dear one. They grieve to a point. Then, early on, the healing spirit sets in. At the same time we can and will rejoice in a different vein. It is difficult to accept God's will when death knocks. But this is also the time when we should take great pride in the good life that the dear person lived and for the fine person the dead was. We celebrate the life the person lived. Here was a person we admired and honored. He or she was always full of love. He or she always cared for those around them. He or she showed their love in many ways, always ready to help and to give. In death we recall often more of the good and more of the noble of the departed, some of which we never even touched on before. We sit back. We think silently within ourselves: What finer qualities could we ask for in a fellow being, particularly when this fellow being was our friend? At this time, racing in our mind are some of our own failings, our own inadequacies. We move on, hoping that in future we will touch more than ever the good of others during their lives around us.

For some of our friends, life is an unfinished symphony which they were in the midst of composing, building on, fine-tuning and finishing, not necessarily making the music a classic. For some, the composition was much nearer completion, even though it was far from perfect in the standards of the world. We admire them all for the good they were able to do. We memorialize the dead, not because they are dead, but for the persons they were and for the joy they brought into this world. Death is not only a loss forever. Death is not only grief. Death is just as much the recall of the joy in the life the dear friend lived. In sorrow we can find strength, when all else seems destroyed around us. We take comfort in the fact that death when it came may have been inevitable. Our friend has gone from us, gone to another world. May our friend find peace forever! We salute our friend, and we rejoice in our friend's life.

BREAK THE BAD NEWS

B ad news is inevitable when it comes. It can come directly to you, or someone can convey it to you. When it comes directly to you, it can be more devastating if your temperament and composure cannot sustain it, or you cannot be humanly accommodating. If someone brings it to you, there is a shield or a barrier that can temporarily, even for a few brief moments, be made to work for you and with you.

We can break bad news with tact, with dignity. Bad news is always a serious matter, and there are times when we can soften the blow and control some of the damage it brings in its wake. To be the messenger of bad news is always a daunting task. If the bad news is death, the thought of conveying such news brings a sense of anxious horror to the bearer of the unhappy tidings.

We have to begin by preparing ourselves, by silently within oneself rehearsing our act in breaking the bad news. We have to begin with a fuller and deeper understanding of the mind of our listener or of all our listeners and their personalities and those who might be directly concerned with or affected by the bad news.

A strong sense of skill and the knowledge of diplomacy in human relations have to be used in conveying the bad news.

Whenever possible, prepare the recipients for the critical stage of the news content. Do not understate, dramatize or over-dramatize the news or the scenario. Equip yourself to be in a position to respond in the best way you can to the listeners' inquiries, their observations, their comments and their concerns, and any request they may express for help in their particular situation.

No one wants to be the messenger of bad news. No one would seek the opportunity. This is not a task that anyone willingly wants to undertake. The news can bring emotional distress and confusion. There are times when, without warning, the situation confronts us, and we have to know how to address it. The harsh realities of life overtake us. Bad news takes its toll on all of us. When the role of the messenger of bad news is thrust on us, we have to learn to bear with ability and with propriety this responsibility in life. We have to be more humble in the process, and it is imperative on us to take control of every situation that we become responsible for. This becomes a test of ourselves, our compassion to help others in their tragedy and their pain.

LIFE IS A WAITING GAME

L ife is a maze, complex and intriguing. Many of us wish it could be more simple. If life was simple, perhaps it could lose some of its glamour, some of its fascination, some of its appeal, much of its wonderment.

Our sights in life can be set in one of these three ways. We can approach life in a constructive fashion. In the second direction, we can be without much purpose or plan. Thirdly, we can do little to positively change life's course or its content. In all this, in many, many ways life is a waiting game for the ordinary things and for the not-so-ordinary things in life. It does not matter who we are or what our station in life is. We can be young; we can be old. We can be royalty; we can be poor. We can wield power; we can be without influence or control. Regardless of our station in life, the waiting game can and does take toll of all of us in different measures and in different situations.

What is the waiting game? There is so much in life that is not instantaneous or prompt or at our command. There is so much or so little happening when we want it to, or when it is best for us that it should happen. The pattern can change every day, and many times during the day. We want things to happen. They do not always happen when we want them to.

At times, we receive a quick answer to life situations. Many times, we do not. It can be a long wait. It can be a short wait. The wait can be inconsequential. The wait can have serious effects on our life and on the lives of those around us. We cannot hasten the passage of time or hasten events or the sequence of happenings. When the wait ends, the outcome can go in a number of directions. It could have been an agonizing wait. The end of the wait can bring disappointment, sadness, pain and suffering. The end of the wait can bring joy with prizes of satisfaction, of accomplishment. The wait can be rewarding.

As we travel the road from childhood, we develop new skills to live in the demands of the waiting game. Every year can add to our skills. Some of these skills are within us, and we have not only to nurture the seedlings but to cultivate them and develop them, preferably over and above the required level for our station in life.

There are small things in life. We wait — at supermarket checker stands, in bank teller lines, for bureaucracy to move to action, in traffic gridlock, in medical doctors' offices, in hospitals for service, at airports for arrival and departure flights, in queues for a number of services in public places. In some cultures and in some countries, waits are the normality in the pattern of life. People frown upon them, but the people remain helpless. They live every day in this surrender. In certain societies, multiple priorities have to be managed. In too many societies, the most damaging aspect of the wait occurs when those in authority are to provide some of the ordinary service to people. In these societies the public is treated as the servant of the bureaucracy and not the reverse roles. Most of these waits are not of damaging and lasting consequences, and they have to be accepted as part of the living pattern. Fortunately, these waits are not the most critical phases of the people's lives.

There are many more important things in life for which we wait. At times, we cannot understand why the wait is long and excruciating. We wait for a task to be done, for a friend to arrive, for a loved one to reach us. We wait for the day and the time for a particular event to happen. We chafe at the restrictions and the confines imposed on us. We wait for the day when friendship with another begins to blink its first indicators. We wait for the day when we can see movement towards reconciliation in a souring relationship that we want to preserve. We wait for time to heal wounds, to overcome difficulties, to solve problems, to find answers to complex issues. We want wounds to heal overnight or sooner. Then, we wait for the time to bring us rewards, successes and positive solutions to all that is in our path.

There are basics and fundamentals in our life, some of which we do not accept, but we have to live with in the game of life. Among these are delays, postponements, action deferred, or happenings not occurring. What does waiting teach us? It teaches us patience, respect, tolerance and endurance. It makes us aware of the realities in other people's lives, and within us steadily develops an understanding of others and of ourselves. It molds certain aspects of our personality and our character. As we move on in life, we become more accommodating in the waiting game. We learn to control and to moderate a self-righteous temper. We wait patiently for opportunities for growth and for a sense of satisfaction to come our way, even if this takes days, weeks and years. Waiting over which we have no control should be respected in a constructive fashion.

The sequences in life's situations are not structured in an orderly fashion for many of us. In the more serious phases of life, we wait and fate keeps moving. We cannot hasten the end of the wait, we cannot hold back or delay the movement or accelerate the happening. There are many events which move fast and the pace gains momentum. Before long the wait is over. Your chance to do differently can be fading away and the wait can be over.

Life teaches us innovative approaches to issues and problems. How much of our lifetime is spent waiting? As long as the time spent is not excessive, not largely uncontrollable and not frequent and not hurting our living pattern, it will not make us grow bone weary. In all this, we know that there are times when we have waited long enough, waited much too long. We cannot overextend the waiting period. We will individually be the best judges of this. The goal is to make the wait not damaging or destructive to our life. We can do this constructively, and we will.

DIFFERENCES SHOULD
BE A PLUS

Differences exist in real life and in the human mind. We can dwell on these differences. We can emphasize them, we can ignore them, we can accept them, we can rebel about them. In yet another way, we can look at them in a positive manner with a constructive approach. Unfortunately, we can often hurt ourselves and hurt others when differences urge us to action, and we then proceed to act in a negative fashion.

A host of reasons can cause differences between people. The differences can be individual characteristics, be they physical, mental, emotional, ideological or psychological. They can emerge in education and training, in career success, in social acclaim and in many, many other details.

Differences can exist on the basis of skin pigmentation. We are born in a different ethnic origin. We are brown, we are black, we are yellow, we are white. We have a less pronounced hue or we are somewhere in between. Some of us are tall, some are short. Some of us are plump, some are slender. Some are beautiful and handsome, some have less of the glamour of life. Some have a great smile to greet others, some remain glum even when they meet friends. We meet people who are unrestrained and effusive in some of their contacts. We are different in our attitudes, in our expressions.

These are not the only differences. There are other dissimilarities that exist for all to see. There are variations in ethics and in our conduct. Our moral standards may be significantly different or they may be a shade different. There are differences of religion between peoples and in religious beliefs and practices. There are differences in the intensity of worship and in the practice of our faith. The manner in which we live our religion can sometimes be evident in our everyday life. With the required guidance, we must search for a formative self-building approach to our religion. We must do this without pressure from those in authority or from those in our social circle. Some of the problems in life today can be traced to the manner in which we live our religion or the way we ban religion from our life.

Differences continue. We must learn to respect people regardless of where they stand on the social scale and the economic ladder. The fact that you or they are low on the scale or at the bottom of the ladder or at the top does not make any of us a worse human being or a better human being. Not all people at the top are super. There are good people at the bottom, at the top and in between. World acclaim, society approval and affluence do not always make us great people. It is our everyday conduct, our temperament, our approach to life, our relations with our fellow beings that make the difference. Even when there is no such or related difference between us, we cannot conceal jealousy if this has gained root within us. We should not exploit people. We should not use resentment, anger and violence against others who are in any way different from us and different from our thinking about humanity.

Life abounds in differences. Life is a mystery, but there is no negative connotation in this concept of differences. It is an enigma in the sense of an adventure. Life becomes and can be an assembly of unexplained differences, differences that can always be made a plus. Each of us can be a creator of the plus from our differences. As we have seen from our own day to day encounters, life is a perplexing array of differences that can promote and encourage us into making differences a positive aspect of life. Despite all this, life is a mystery of differences and all of us must live in a way that can result in making life together constructively and happily in our family, in our community and in our society. We must portray life making differences to be significant positives in life. Differences exist and will remain with us. They should be made a plus in everyday life.

OUR LIMITATIONS

As humans, our genes gave us our first limitations. They were with us at birth. As we go on in life we overcome some or many of these limitations, and, regrettably, on occasion we add new limitations. This is a sector on the path of our human development.

Some of our limitations stem from our own person, and who we are, and what we make of ourselves. As we grew from childhood to adult life and beyond, much that happened in our life left its mark on us, at times an indelible mark. This impact can be good, and, maybe in some respects, it can be not-so-good. The not-so-good creates some of the additional limitations and some of the unwanted limitations we experience in life.

In this land of our limitations, we can dream. We can get our imagination in action. We can assess and reassess the situation. We can begin to plan. We can get into becoming a high energy person, with achievement as our record, or we can taper off into mediocrity and even be relegated into oblivion.

Many of us can be empowered, and not be overpowered by our limitations. Have faith, an undying faith in ourselves. Project this faith for all the world to see. Build on it, but do not be boastful or even arrogant. The world will find it easy to reject us if we appear arrogant of who we are. The opportunity reservoir may be drained dry without limitations, but we can be very determined to bring about change.

Our life depends on what we want to do, and how much of this is in the area of the achievable. The goal may be small, but significant. On the other hand, the goal may be big, too close to the summit. What is crucial, is our ability to control our sense of purpose, and to achieve the attainable. We may be loaded with talent, we may and can have limitations, but unless we take action our potential for achievement is purposeless. We must be cognizant of our human limitations. We have to grow towards perfection.

Regrettably, in the perceived knowledge of our limitations, too many among us sit back, and we resign, we surrender to the power of our limitations. These merciless limitations grip us. They disturb us. They overpower us. They snatch from us our ambitions, our desires, and even from our needs.

As we said earlier, limitations are a part of our humanity. We must internalize and recognize those limitations which cannot be removed from our life. We should see if we can work around them, and do something constructive with them. We should seek and find comfort if at times the incorrigible element of helplessness has taken abode in us. In the same vein we should externalize, and in the process, capitalize on our potential and our strengths.

The feeble impotence of our own human limitations saddens some of us. If we have done all we can to overcome the limitations, and we have not succeeded, then we have to learn to accept this situation, and to live with it. A day will dawn when our spirit and our desire to achieve will soar. We will accept our limitations, we will work constructively, and we will soon revel at our success. We will not dwell on our failures and our inabilities. Our limitations will no longer hamper our growth and our accomplishments. In all life's challenges, we will remember to use our talent, however limited, however confined. We will be reinforced in our thinking that nobody can take away our ability from us, not even our limitations in ability. We will recognize that our limitations will not be our undoing in life.

7.09

Drain the Dregs of Bitterness and Hatred

From time immemorial, the world in its evil has not changed for the better in some of its intensity, in its command over the scope of the life of the people. We should not be a part of this evil. In some aspects evil has reduced, in other aspects it has increased and in yet others it has remained the same. The reason the intensity of evil still abounds in people stems largely from misguided individuals.

The presence of evil in society is disappointing. It can be devastating. Life has many characteristics. One of these is that as a people, we are all different. Many, many are good. We contribute in our conduct and through our way of life to the happiness of those around us. Then there are some that portray the negative aspects of humanity. One of these negatives is the bitterness and hatred which enter our life in a variety of situations and circumstances.

Many times bitterness and hatred emerge from inadequacies within us. We find ourselves on a lower plane in society. We do not accept the accomplishments of others. We cannot reconcile ourselves to the fact that others have made the most of the opportunities that have come astride in their path. We chafe at the restrictions — real and imaginary — imposed on ourselves. Self-discipline within us ceases to prevail. We detect bias in our attitude. We do not always brush this bias aside. The cost of pain and suffering takes toll within us. We may be doomed to failure in more than one aspect of life, because we are enveloped or partly embroiled in bitterness and hatred.

The enemy is not society. It is not our culture. Often it is not our family or our friends. It is we ourselves as individuals. We may be chin deep in problems. Bitterness and hatred will not be the solution, and these two elements need not even be on the path to the solution. We can walk away with bitterness and hatred as our companions, or we can turn around, reject bitterness and hatred, seek the constructive side of life, and fight back. We will do best to take the latter as the first step. We will discover that in this constructive mode we come to accept others, and in the process others accept us, despite all our faults and our shortcomings, as many as these may be.

Hatred comprises a strong dislike and ill-will. Bitterness can be harsh, severe, piercing in its depth. It is characterized by strong feelings of hatred, resentment and cynicism.

As a first step on the road to recovery, we adopt a positive outlook. We remain poised. We want to move away from our experiences and from being immersed in the unhealthy and cruel mode. We begin by setting an initial goal to drain the dregs of bitterness and hatred from our life. New visions supersede the less promising present. We feel confident that success will come to the seekers of success. We face fear when it appears in front of us, or is not too far in the distance. In our resolve in new visions, fear will disappear. We have taken possession of a new key to life. The new key, particularly in our approach to others and our feeling for others, finds its abode in our mind, in our outlook and in all life situations. The new key is with us in all our challenges. We can and we must destroy our enemy which is bitterness and hatred. We will then soon be riding high for the best in life.

TIME IS NOT ON OUR SIDE

In all the world there are certain things we cannot buy in any transaction, in any market, in any phase of life. One of these is Time. Not only can we not buy Time, we cannot even trade Time. No one can give it to us now or in the future, or give it back to us from the past. Time cannot be replaced; it cannot be recaptured. Time lost at any time is Time lost forever.

Relentless is the march of Time. It cannot be stopped in its stride. Time does not wait for us, regardless of who we are, king or pauper, saint or sinner. We see the minutes tick away, the hours of the day speed by. The years are soon over. We can pause to ponder over the power of Time, and even in this phase we are spending Time. Time stares all of us in the face all our waking hours. When we are asleep it does not stop. It does not take a break. It moves on. It is said that counting time is not as crucial as making time count. We should not have it said of us that we did not blink an eye as time raced by.

Time affects each of us every moment of our life. It is not a commodity, it is not a possession. Time, as it affects each of us, is like nothing else on this good earth. It influences all our activity and all our inactivity. Sheer indulgence in the less wanted in life should not be a drain on our Time.

So let us spring forward to put Time to productive use. Let us derive benefit from it as much as we can. Let us remember that it is priceless. Let us be prudent in its use. Time can become a luxury, which we possessed yesterday, but today we do not have the same two hours of yesterday.

Youth and the years that follow are always a time of wonder. Time should not be wasted when we are young. It should not be wasted when we are not young. It makes many of us grieve whenever we see it wasted by ourselves or by others. Adlai Stevenson said that it is not years in your life that count. It is the life in your years. How true this statement has been, and always will be!

We can be constructive in the utilization of Time. Time can be measured in several forms. It need not be all in work, or all in fun, or all in enjoyment, in creativity or in earning money. Some of it can be sitting back and relaxing. Some of it can be deep in thought, in contemplating, in meditating, in formulating plans.

As we have said earlier, we have to use Time in a constructive fashion. Time can be our counsellor. Get ahead of Time, not behind it. As Time goes on, we should be able to commend ourselves on the productive use of our Time, hoping that most of our life has been devoted to the creative.

Let us find Time to enjoy the glory of life, not forgetting the simplest of things — the fresh beauty of the color-adorned flowers, the blaze of the setting sun, sheep grazing as they huddle in the rolling green of the mountainside, the majesty of the rich blue sea breaking on the white sandy shores, we standing nestled close together on the farm bridge while the blue-green water flows in its tranquility beneath us. There are many more beautiful, heavenly scenes. Let us not for the want

214 Maurice Gracias

of Time miss any of these wonders of nature or the wonders of the people of this world.

Time is a precious commodity. Hour after hour, day after day, year after year Time marches on. Not one of us can control it. None of us can re-live Time that passed on to the end a little while ago, a day ago or a month ago, or Time that passed on a long time ago, again to eternity.

The golden rule is to always keep Time on our side, work to keep Time on our side. Our implementation of the rule should be much more than an attempt. It should be a firm purpose, followed by determined action. This will make all the difference in our life. We want to live life to the fullest. Every minute of Time, every second of Time in life are forever irreplaceable and unrepeatable. If we have discovered how Time will work for us, we can make it work for us. Then, we will not be and we cannot be beaten in this battle with Time.

WORK FOR
MASTERY IN LIFE

CAN WE LOVE WORK?

For too many people, the word "work" is sometimes synonymous with the word "nightmare". Too many among us hate work. They despise it, they detest it, they avoid it wherever and whenever and however they can. But for just as many people, work haunts them. They do their work out of sheer necessity, for the agreed money they receive in compensation for their labors. There is a smaller group of people who love their work. They enjoy it, they derive satisfaction from it. Work brings us satisfaction and money. We all need money, since society has always functioned with the medium of money. If we could receive compensation in the form of money and goods and services through any other means save work, most of us would not work.

Work is a critical component in life. Work is seen by most people to be a bore. Some people work most days of the week, if not every working day. Most work under supervision, under guidance, under surveillance at different levels and to a different degree. They have to conform; they cannot be enterprising or innovative, except to a minimal degree. Work becomes repetitious and monotonous. They long to get away from this employer-afflicted or self-afflicted drudgery. They want to do other things that might capture and hold their interest. If, however, incentives are given for superior quality output and high productivity, work takes on varying degrees of fulfillment for many of us. Work takes on even a greater sense of satisfaction when there is fulfillment and reward from enterprising and innovative direction and performance.

There is much we can learn from the people who love work, who enjoy work. They keep themselves motivated. They may or may not be addicted to work. Some work by relaxing at work, at the same time accomplishing at work. Work is not all bad, and work is not to be hated. Steer clear of the decay in deportment, in the attitude that work is to be hated. Individually, we can make for a good attitude to our work. In the same context, we can make for a bad attitude.

We can even love work, if we make it interesting and exciting. We can look forward to performing at work. We can view it as challenging. We can see it as bringing our many faculties into play. We can make use of knowledge and skills acquired in training for the particular job or in other training we have undergone. In a mental and emotional sense, we can make work intensely rewarding.

Work discovers talents and builds skills. Work separates the men from the little boys, the women from the little girls. Work sees the workers grow in stature, advance in the hierarchy of the organization. Some of us can squander the early part of our lives and our careers, and the growing promise of the future. The career we create is ours; the job we work in is the employer's.

There is an aspect of life that is repeated among people. Often we hear it said, "Thank God, it's Friday!" We should rather want people to say, "Where did the week go?" or better still, "Thank God, it has been a great week!"

The worker sees goals being achieved, ambitions being

realized, new dreams being formulated, and in the process the imagination is fired up. In this atmosphere, in this frame of mind, we as workers excel ourselves. We climb to new heights. Some reach the pinnacle of human endeavor. We innovate, we improvise, we invent, and we could not have done all this without a strong love for work and the philosophizing of work and its purpose in achievement. Sometimes a genius is born in the process of the work environment. A passion for excellence is born and nurtured.

Woman's and man's God-given talent and brilliance evolve in many ways. One of these is through work and the application of our abilities, all in different measure and in different fields of endeavor. Some people, therefore, grow to love work. The greatness of individuals and of nations emerges through the medium of work and through work fulfillment. Work allows us to bathe in the glory of success and of triumph.

Work would be more rewarding for all of us if we were not concerned about what is going to happen, but instead, of what we could make happen. This attitude, this approach would create a world of difference in our lives.

Believe in what you are doing, and experience a strong sense of joy doing it. In time, you will come to a realization that it is so much fun to go to work. Do not just stay in step. Set the stage for solid growth. You set the pace, you explore new horizons, and you can love your work. You will perform at peak levels. You will inspire yourself to take on new challenges. Do not allow the process of reaching the top to overpower you. Motivate fellow-workers and, if you are in authority, do not manipulate them. Boost their self-esteem. Work together as colleagues and, at times, as competitors. Promote new thinking, new applications of concepts, new attitudes.   Push your career into high gear.   Your strategy should be to persuade.   It should not be to coerce.

For many, we recognize that a large sector of our life is spent at work.   Let us all do better at our work.   Let us begin by taking pride in our work.   Let this pride grow into love for our work.   None of this will come easy.   But the more we love our work, the more fulfilling will be our life.   It will not just be time spent at work, merely for completing our work.   We will soon come to a realization that in the process of a career we work to reinforce our feelings of self-worth.   We can love work and derive fulfillment of needs and of satisfaction.

Work and its accomplishments can give us one of our greatest sources of happiness in life, and striving for this goal should make all of us do all we can to love work.

MONEY AND ITS POWER

Money plays an important and decisive part in our lives. It is the essence of business, and in some critical ways it is at the fundamental of human relations and human activities. Down the centuries in the lives of people, money translates into resources and wealth. It has been the one crucial factor, sometimes the most crucial factor in life, next to good health and happiness.

Money has provided the purchasing power for all our material needs and our human needs. If you have all the money you want, you can, with two exceptions, have all you want and more. The two exceptions are that you may not have all the good health and all the happiness you want. If you have money sufficient for your needs and if you have the ability to regulate and control the flow of cash resources, money does not become an issue for you. But if you have little or insufficient money or no money, and your needs and desires go unmet, the unavailability of money and the inability to satisfy your needs create problems, many a time problems of serious dimensions.

As we all know, money does not grow on trees. It is not found in the streets, even those streets supposedly revered in absentia as paved with gold. It has to be earned chiefly from the fruits of our labor and from the skill and the intelligence within our command. In conjunction with this, there are different methods and different skills to manage money and to make money grow. Money can also flow from an inheritance, from capital accumulated from our endeavors and from a lucky spin. In all this, money management and investment expertise become crucial.

The cardinal rule to remember concerning money is that you should never allow money to control you. You should be in total command. Do not be overpowered by money. The ability and the expertise in managing money may take time and skill to achieve, but come about it will. You have to have the resolve and the dedication and the persistence to manage money, and you must continue to always build on the knowledge to do this in a changing world.

You may develop the competence to control money through your own skill. You may do this from a study of the principles and the techniques pertaining to the subject and through a study of your environment and the world you live in. You may do this by gaining close familiarity with the whys and the wherefores of money. You could do this through a trusted friend or through knowledge from books and happenings in the world around you. Above all, begin by learning to exercise self-discipline in the realm of money. In time, you will generate not only more money than you ever had before, but you will learn how to spend more than you ever did before, and you will do so prudently. In doing all this, you will still have even more money resources left over.

As life moves on, none of us should have to scratch for a living. Open today a window to the expanse of a new world. Unlock your creativity. Tap the creativity and the ingenuity of others, without abusing their rights, their confidentiality and their privacy. There is always a cycle of challenge and of opportunity.

Not all those who excel in school make money. School develops in us education and skills to perform in different occupations and to earn money. School does not teach us to manage the money we earn, or the money we have. Managing money successfully brings into life the power of money.

Do not be enslaved by money. If you have the ability, you will attain the ultimate in money management. It will not be easy. You may need counsel. In order to make your money, you can use other people's money through prudent borrowing, and you can avail of other people's brainpower through advice and guidance you properly seek.

Money will not control you or your lifestyle, unless you succumb to this pattern. You can and will control money, and if you have that control, money will do what you want it to do for you. In the money game, you in control will experience the finest hour for you. It can leave you free to enjoy all the many other blessings of a good life.

Unfortunately, very few people understand money, and fewer still have a strong desire to persist in acquiring a skill in this field. As a consequence, the personal scarcity of money continues to control the lives of so many of us. But there are a sizable few people in total control of money. Money is their slave and not their Master. We salute those in control. Can more of us follow their path of accomplishment and justified pride? Can more of us master Money? We can if we have the skill to manage money, and develop the power that comes from Money.

ACHIEVEMENT CAN
BE OURS

9.01

A Life Achieving, Achieving......

L ife is a mystery, at times of infinite proportions. In one's life, there are many interesting times, many exciting moments, many events of joy, many perplexing episodes. There are good times, there are not-so-good times. We are not to sit content with only one, or a very few achievements. We do not want to go through life under-utilized or underperforming. We can live a life that is barren, without hope. We may have made this choice by not wanting to live a constructive, a productive life. Those of us who do this tend to blame everybody and anybody, but ourselves. Our ambition should be a life achieving and achieving. Hopefully, the person within us senses this and moves into the ambition of growth and accomplishment.

Even when we have experienced negatives in our life, we should not dwell on them for any prolonged length of time. We should analyze the causes of the negatives, and be alert to possible repetition. We cannot achieve on a plan in the absence of a plan. We must assume the positive attitude. We have to learn to be resilient. If we give ourselves the time, we can and we will change our lives.

For our life, early on, we should develop a road map. We can formulate a schedule defining clear objectives within some time zones, but not zones set in rigid, inflexible time periods. We should not rush the process. We should look into all aspects of refining the process. The objectives and the time zones must not be unrealistic, and they should be subject to periodical review. In many situations, there are no guidelines in the areas we are seeking to pursue our goals, particularly when we embark on a voyage of discovery and the ocean is uncharted. We cannot overlook the dimensions of our decisions in the vast expanse of the ocean before us.

The world is brimful of opportunity for the person who wants to go in search of the opportunity. That person will find it. There are times when we bring in new sustaining energy to renew our resolve. Creative talent must not be satisfied by everyday routine. We must unleash our creativity. Our body language must gain prominence and be prevailing and convincing.

We can discover much within ourself and triumph in the fruits of the discovery. We may have to change our priorities. Our signposts should be established as soon as possible. As early as we can, we should aim to reach our full potential, and with this goal we should be in the ambit of our expectations. We should never underestimate the value of other people, other programs or other events.

We must raise our consciousness for achievement. Within us, we have an inner sense that we should listen to. When we feel powerless, we should show faith in our capability. We have to stay abreast of our competition and manifest the ability to claim attention and to draw power. More of us should have the ability to excel under pressure. We have to eliminate fear from our life.   We have to be aware of the danger of failure when ambition overfeeds our ability and our resources.   We may founder. We begin to ponder the consequences. We have to beat the odds.   We do so in the conviction that we can achieve.   We should emerge as an individual in pursuit of a vision.

It can be disheartening to try to achieve and to not achieve, but it is a tragedy to fail because we do not even attempt when we have the ability to or the motivation to achieve.   Plan to succeed.   Do not resign yourself to where destiny, without intervention from you, may take you.

The fountain of youth has nothing to do with age.   For some the fountain has no flow, not even a drip, even when they are young, and presumed to be flowing with energy. Then there are others who discover the fountain of youth in their lives many times, not only in their younger days, but as time moves on into the once distant horizon. They can and do advance in their chronological age by maybe 15 and 25 years, but they do not abandon the fountain of youth.

Some do not achieve, because they are so occupied making a bare living and not finding the time to make a life of quality for themselves.   We must change in order to achieve. Prominence must be given to our creativity, our resourcefulness, our adaptability, our intuitiveness.   We must be self-seeking in a positive manner.   We can be graceful and majestic and not be brazen as we do this.

In life the world of achieving enchants, fascinates, mysti-fies and captivates us.   Our intellect, our sense of purpose and our intensity, our dedication become the determining elements.   We must integrate the faith in ourselves with our plan and our work on it. When all is said and done, recognize and acknowledge your accomplishments. Feel honored by them. In all modesty, wear your badge of glory. The glory is yours and only yours, to be won, as Winston Churchill said, through blood, sweat and tears. Again, in all the bounty you have earned, be generous to yourself. You will not go unrewarded. Our day by day living, if we purposefully do so, can always make our life A Life Achieving, Achieving.......

———————————————

No Guts, No Glory

No guts, no glory! No risk, no reward! No pain, no gain! Somewhat frightening, somewhat perplexing, in some ways frustrating. Is it not?

How patently true are these first three statements for most of what we know as life's glory, life's reward and life's gain! Many of the great achievements of all time, many of any and all achievements in our own times have come from people with guts, people who took risks, people who foresaw possible pain in the process. Nothing worthwhile, nothing great comes to us on a plate for free. Nothing worthwhile or great comes to us without effort, without sweat, even at times without tears.

Achievements are not random shots at glory, at reward or at gain. These are not flukes or chance happenings. These are not strokes of luck. These are not accidents of fate. They are deliberate and purposeful acts with the singular objective of a fervent desire to accomplish, or with a burning passion to accomplish.

Everything in this realm of accomplishment began on the basis of knowledge, at times little or limited knowledge, situations and circumstances which might have deterred the less determined, the enfeebled. Each endeavor had to be equipped with a specific and detailed awareness of the risks involved, and the strength and the resolve required for the ultimate achievement. We have to accept that if we ignore or miss out on an opportunity, we can lose on our future. We have to work for the self-fulfillment of many of our own concepts. In the process, we may have, at times, to disregard, to set aside traditional thinking.

Once the glow of endeavor, the seeds of awareness, the strength and the resolve are embedded firmly within us, they have to be nurtured and given ground for growth and sustenance. Much of this would come from an objective analysis and evaluation of the risks and the possible rewards. The analysis and the evaluation of each endeavor would come from the individual risk-taker, aided by knowledge acquired from self-study, from books, from friends, from advisors, and even by being alert to those who do not want us to succeed, and at times who even work so that we do not succeed. In these situations, bone-weariness must not set in.

We must develop a decision-making data base in our endeavors. The analysis and the evaluation are almost always a stiff, uphill battle, sometimes doomed to failure. Despite this, we should take comfort in the fact that so many succeed where others succumb against odds. We would like to be a story of success. With some of this effort completed, we now stand at stage one of the Battle for Gain, the Battle for Reward, the Battle for Glory.

If in the assessment, distant or immediate prospects are remote or too far-fetched for favorable results, action moves to the second stage. For our objective and goal, we must now do our own re-evaluation armed with a strong self-critical assessment, and if deemed necessary aided by the advice of a trusted friend.

At this stage, the evaluation may direct us to the decision not to proceed, not to take the risk, either because there will be no gain or reward, monetary or otherwise, or that the benefit will be less than commensurate with the risk. We are at one journey's end, perhaps a short journey, and we must resolve to begin another journey. Remember, do not be turned away by marginal issues, by marginal projections, by anticipations of marginal results. Marginal assessments and results call for more demanding reviews, perhaps repeat reviews with concentration on the more damaging features.

If the result of the evaluation is that we should not proceed, we should not be overly disappointed. Hopefully, we stopped early enough in our tracks. Rather, we pat ourselves on the back for avoiding failure, and for the opportunity to now devote our energies to new projects, new programs and new glory. Assimilate what we have learned from the unproductive, the failed effort on our life's scene. We may have been wrong before, happily this time to discover early enough to avoid being wrong once again.

If the evaluation of the analysis of the project is that there is sufficient reason to proceed with the project, we will begin to reinforce our strength and our resolve to continue with the project.

Be prepared to assemble or to reassemble. Gather together all the resources needed — capital, material and the human effort. Formulate our implementation plan, arrange and re-arrange priorities and proceed. Should we need a confidant with whom to bounce off our ideas and our thoughts, we should not hesitate to seek this friend out.

Once this is in place, be prepared to proceed. Get started with an abundance of enthusiasm. Be dedicated to implementation and competitiveness, at times in the face of fierce competition. We should not stumble when it comes to each one of us believing in ourselves. Glory, Reward and Gain will be ours if our project has been well thought out and implemented. What a sense of triumph, a sense of accomplishment, a sense of happiness and a vindication of our ability to succeed awaits us around the corner! We will have deservedly earned our Glory, our Reward and our Gain. We will stand saluted for our achievements.

9.03

WHAT IS SUCCESS?

Success has been defined in a hundred ways and more. We will look at a few of the broader categories of success. One is achievement in the face of the odds stacked against us, even when there is no human opposition for us to contend with. Another is reaching the top after stumbling almost to ruin after the first few steps. Yet another is discovering ourselves at the summit in a highly competitive atmosphere. Then there is thriving in chaos. Yet another, is when we want to be considered an equal, and in projecting ourselves forward we excel. There are many more.

We can succeed in many fields of endeavor if we have never held ourselves back, if we have not spared ourselves as far as humanly possible. To the maximum extent possible, do not be undercapitalized in power or in resources of any kind. We have to go into life prepared that we may not be successful at the first attempt, or the second attempt or at later attempts. It is up to us to have a burning desire to succeed and to develop a prevailing passion to succeed. We then assess the prospects and measure our strengths. We should keep on plodding.

There are times when opportunity knocks and we choose to ignore the knock. In many of life's situations, it is much easier to say "No" to opportunity, than it is to say "Yes". It is not when we start, but when we finish that matters. If at any stage of our endeavor, we did give a negative response, we should dwell soon on the thinking that prompted our negative reception. In life's complexities, present gratification may have to be deferred for accomplishment at a later date.

Remember that the price of success can be staggering, but not always is. Success can be obtained at a price, but never for nothing. Success can be ours, in some instances if we are able to pay the price on a road that is long, winding and laden with difficulties and obstacles. Many people who achieve success make it on their own. Each of us must assess our strengths and our weaknesses, and from this evaluate the prospects for success. We should not be discouraged by people judging our capability in the negative.

Success can come more rapidly, more forcefully, if the person who becomes the leader has the substance, the flair and the imagination. We must reveal boundless energy in working for success. We must have a commitment to excellence. We need more and more inspiration from within, even an abundance of it. Our strongest natural instinct is to find and to deserve success for ourselves.

Achievement is not only a representation of our capability, but it is a projection of our potential for even greater achievement. Success gives the world a better and a more explicit definition of our image. Let us take our image to the mountaintop. Success is ours, depending on how passionately we want it and strive for it. Nobody, nobody can hold us back or deny us the good of life. We can succeed, if we want to, and if we pursue this goal. We have a mission in life, and the mission is to accomplish, to succeed.

BUDGET FOR SUCCESS

How can we budget for success? When we speak of success in the context of availing of our resources, we do so in the broadest and all-encompassing sense, with worldly material and attendant concerns before us. Success does not always come with or be guaranteed by unlimited resources, such as money, brain power and access to resources for achievement. With all the wealth of resources, we can still fall short on success.

We know that success is not handed out to anyone, not even by those we love, not even those who are dear to us. One has always to earn it, one way or the other. In order to budget for success, we must assemble all our resources and develop our plan of action. We must cultivate an unconcealed penchant to achieve, a sated desire for success.

Our resources include our will power, our brain power, our ability, our access to needed resources, the climate for achievement and, in a large measure, self-discipline. We have to foster a climate which will have the incentives for us. We cannot be adrift. We must be in primary control. We must remain poised in our assessment of the prospects for success. In every difficulty, in every crisis, we may and can discover an opportunity. We must build on our knowledge and our skill. Our performance will grow. Above all, we must communicate intelligence.

We were all born with talent, maybe some talent, maybe a little talent, maybe a good measure of talent. The talent was to be developed. Competence had to grow. Additions to the talent were to be acquired. With all the talent we command, we must seek our stage. When we have found our stage, or we have built a stage, we must embark onto our performance. With the proper insight, the proper controls, a budget will govern our activity.

We need our budget for success. The only reason we fail is that we stop trying. We should not stop trying. We do not expend our budget without concern for success. The world is waiting for you and for me. As we know, in life there is nothing that can be bought without paying a price, and for the success in life and its price we must budget.

SECOND BEST IS NOT GOOD ENOUGH

G ive our best to the world, our very best, not our second best. This is what high achievement demands. Our best, not our second best, is what is most rewarding. The very best is what we should strive for, and, with dedication and steadfastness, we will be amazed as to how often, may be not every single time, we can give our best to ourself and to the world.

Regardless of the magnitude of the task, seek to be a perfectionist, not with a wild, unattainable goal, but with a firm striving and resolve to reach the ultimate on the plane of achievement. We must consider all our opportunities and all our options. We must weigh the affirmatives and the negatives at our level of achievement, and we must make proper judgments. We must pace ourself.

In the world around us we often find that high level achievement and the exacting standards that this demands are abandoned and sacrificed in order to attain the levels of the more easily reached. Far too many of us accept the easy way out. We cut corners, and we do less than is perfect or near perfect. In our task, we may have to risk more than what others consider to be safe or certain of achievement.

As standards waver, the perfectionist may look on, fragmented and wrecked. Sometimes too little is done to uphold the best that is in us. As perfectionists, we could avoid becoming a pain around those who will do with less, but we should not abandon or sacrifice our standards. We should understand that not all of us can reach the same level of achievement, but we should give our best to the world. Too often, we sacrifice our craft, whatever this may be. We tend not to reject or replace flawed work, or work projects that are leading in that direction.

When we strive to attain our best, frustration, trials, disappointment and failure come our way many times, more often than otherwise. Because of the high level to be attained, the possibility of failure stares us in the face. Depending on our frame of mind, these experiences can do remarkable things to us. They can steel us to be unbeatable. On the other side, they can shatter us. We can be destroyed.

Too many of us go through life, not in deliberate, purposeful steps. We slide through life with minimal or some little effort and resolve, thinking little, doing little, fearful of most things, ignorant of many aspects in life and dubious of even others. We encounter so many of these people around us. Fear of failure has gripped them. They are timid and even cowardly of venturing into the realm of the unknown.

Overcome earlier challenges, earlier setbacks, and in us will grow the confidence to go on. We will not stop at second best. We will not display combativeness. We will not be swamped in. A word of caution is to be heeded. When the situation warrants, we recall the well-known saying: Measure three times, and cut once.

242 Maurice Gracias

When we do not do enough to give our best to the world, we will either be doing second best or not succeeding. We are to be reminded again and again that we should never settle for second best. Doubt and suspicion and fear should not bar our progress. Too easily we overlook the one who dares, wins and wins at the highest level. In a constructive mode, discontent with our past performance can be one way of opening for us the avenue to progress and achievement.

Success does not just happen. We create it. We have to play to win to the topmost, and not to play to lose. We must instill and cultivate within our innermost selves the principles of win-win strategies. Persistence can change us. We plod on. We become doubly resolute. We build an environment that is stimulating, motivating and challenging. We draw on our inner self. We must put our creativity, our intelligence and our ability to work. Our one goal should be to fulfill a carefully formulated and properly studied plan. Soon we begin to give our best. We see among us some who are on the road to becoming young geniuses in a hurry. As human as we are, in these circumstances, this is only to be expected. These are the people for whom Second Best is not Good Enough. Let us urge ourselves to be resolute, to be unwavering, to do all we can to be one of them, one of the Best, the very Best.

9.06

REACH FOR THE STARS

There are many stars high above in the firmament of heaven. Lower down in our own firmament there are also stars, separate and distinct from the stars in the firmament of heaven. In our little world, in our not-so-little world, we can reach for the stars. Whether times have been difficult or times have been blessed with achievement, what counts most is not what lies behind us but what lies ahead of us. We must have a goal we believe in, and we must support it all the way.

In the deep secrecy of their own mind, many successful people are amazed at their own ability for achievement. In retrospect and in the privacy of their own thinking, they marvel at their accomplishments. They attempt to analyze their prowess, their faith in themselves, their perseverance. They know they have worked unflinchingly to make their dreams a reality. They know that there were times when failures and discouragement stood in their path, and problems and setbacks almost made them lose hope for a better, a finer tomorrow. But the will and the dedication to be their best, to do their best did not desert them. They were not just motivated and encouraged to get to the top; they made themselves firmly possessed by their conviction.

At all stages in our life we must reach for the stars. Within us there is faith and hope, there is potential, there is promise. We cannot reconcile ourselves to nonperformance, to mediocrity. We must not be crippled by disappointment, by defeat. Even if we do not attain stardom, we will have the lesser satisfaction, satisfaction all the same, of having strived to reach for the stars, and in the process we will have produced a measure of accomplishment. We do not yield to the less performing.

Some of us see a trend and we jump on the bandwagon. Whenever the bandwagon is not within sight, we must move with our creative urge. We must demonstrate consistently our commitment to excellence. We will strive to remain undaunted by failures. We come to believe that often what is dubbed by others as impossible, is possible for us. If we know the rules, we can work to comply with the rules or find the way around the rules without an abuse of another's power. When such is the confidence within us, we can do almost all we want. We can act as the catalyst in a decision-making environment.

When we have talent, and success comes our way, our responsibilities and challenges multiply. We work hard and move up the scale. We attempt more than just work to make our creativity reach a climax every day. Repeat this day after day. Bring into play our mind and all our talent and all our skill, because we can lose these if we do not use them. We become poorer for the loss, and so is the world around us. Cultivate always the spirit of wanting to do better. Focus on what we do best. Soon we will know what it is to be the best.

Climb the ladder to the stars, be it one, three or five or more steps at a time. We soon learn that all our individual resources are bound for the stars. In the process, we come to a realization that we can reach the stars, and that we can do so with style and with grace. We must dare to be different, dare to be the finest, dare to be at the topmost rung of the ladder. We must dare to be not less than the best, and we can create an incredible future for ourselves. If we believe that we can do anything we want within reason, we will discover that in reality we can. Before long, we will find that we have excelled under pressure. We will conclude that when our goal is to Reach for the Stars, we cannot and should not argue with success. And Reach the Stars we will.

TAKE CREDIT FOR YOUR SUCCESS

Amongst us are people who stand on the rooftop and crow. They look for the limelight, not necessarily related to a particular achievement, not because they have something significant to offer the world, but because they want to be seen, to be noticed, to be recognized, to be acknowledged. They even shout aloud about their successes, their triumphs, their achievements. They do this even when in some cases their work and their efforts do not really qualify to be designated under the term Success. They are a success but not more than an ordinary accomplishment.

But then there are many, many people who do not talk about their successes, or boast about their successes, or even make a deliberate attempt to proclaim their accomplishments to the outside world. These people are unassuming, they are not conceited. Among them are also those who harbor lingering doubts of their greatness. Best of all there are those who live in modesty, acknowledging within themselves their accomplishments.

People in high places get substantial credit for their successes, regardless of the nature and the impact of their achievements.

These people have the media and the public following to acclaim them. Those not in high places do not have these agents to announce them. As such, many times too many do not get credit for their success. We can cite occasions when people tend to ignore deliberately the success of others, mainly out of jealousy. These people sidestep the success of others, they belittle others.

We must give credit to others for their success, for their accomplishment. Then, we must take credit for our own successes, for our accomplishments. We must do so in all modesty, and without being overbearing. We must not worship unduly our own achievements, our own prominence in society. We can build on our success when we inwardly within ourselves take credit for our achievements. The thrill of success lives within us. We must remember that birds sing without applause, and we should learn that many a time we can do the same. In all this worldly parade, we can share our fascination for success with those around us, taking credit for our success, without unduly applauding ourselves.

PEOPLE AROUND US

Every Face Has A Story

Behind every face in this world, there is many a story to narrate. Some of it is a story of the present. Some of it is a story of the past, including at times glimpses of the ancestral past. It is a story of that particular face's earlier past, the immediate past and a reflection of the present. It has also some portrayal of times yet to come. It is a story some of us want to tell, or it could be a story we would not want anyone to know, or anyone to narrate on our behalf. In our own story, each one of us wants to be selective in what we want the world outside to know or our inner circle to know, and, even rightly so, we do not want the world to dwell upon all or any specific part of our story. We make the choice of the road we want to travel, and we choose the journey we are on.

Everyone of the stories on the faces around is so different, so unique, so special, so unlike what we visualize, even if we imagine our past and our present to be closely identical to or nearly the same as someone around us. We may think the stories are the same, but on analysis they are not. At times, they do not even closely resemble each other. From our first days in this world, we received the individual ability to respond in our own secret way to people we relate to and to life's events. To a large extent, we strive to fashion our own lives, but we do not always succeed in our dedication and in our endeavors.

We are faced with a fascinating narration of the past, and we are provided some less glaring insight into the future. Some faces tell a story of childhood joy and healthy positive abandon. They tell of the magnificence of achievement, success and maturity, with all the deliberate preparedness that goes for adulthood. Some faces tell of childhood sadness, and being not wanted and not loved. Many have been themselves raised with love in their home, while others have grown their own separate way unloved and uncared, maybe even rejected. Yet others have grown not knowing their home as a home with all its virtues and with all its blessings. For some the teen years have been challenging and fulfilling, and with these years have come in all majesty and grandeur the humility, the maturity, the pride and the self-respect of life. For others the years have been frustrating with little or no building of character, no building of resolve and no preparation for a productive and rewarding adulthood. These adolescent stages can leave their mark — not always, we pray, a damaging mark — on the human face and on the human mind and soul. Adulthood will be affected and influenced by all this, unless corrections are made with speed and with resolution. We have to stem the drift, once we detect it.

The story on the faces of many around us can be one of gladness, happiness and success. These particular people give us a strong, constructive approach to life. They present a befitting posture, humble and sincere. On the face of many of them, the law of civility reigns supreme. On the other hand, the story on the face of some others can be one of disappointment, failure and sorrow. In many cases the faces we see had their molds given substantial shape and form as they stood on the threshold of adult life.

As we move on, as the march of life continues, we see fear, sadness, desperation and anger present. Much of the bad and much of the good is created by our interaction with others and our having to cope with the unavoidable, or something that we or others are unable or unwilling to channel in a positive direction. For some it has been a case of not wanting to fight adversity and difficulty, and we remain in wait for self-pity as we feel it can emerge from others. There are those who are shattered by rejection. Some faces reflect life experiences and life changes that are non-accusatory. Others wear a sour personality. We see the blend in the complexion. All these people exist around us. They do not live the good life that could be theirs, a good life that could be theirs even without them being royalty or affluent or on top of the world.

In every face, young and not so young, we can see a story, at times a story so different from the stories of many around. Sometimes it is a commingling of the good and the bad. For some there is much good; for others it is mostly bad or all bad. There is joy and happiness behind the face of those who received the good as this face marches on. You see the dream of success in the eyes of many. There is a feeling of wonder and amazement. Without this feeling of wonder and amazement, the face can be devoid of the magnificence of life.

How full of wonder and glory life is! What a story lies behind every face! Let us do something every day to make the story behind our own face even more positive and even more constructive than it is today. We can succeed if we will do right. As more of us do this, our own society and the world will be a richer and a better place for us all. Among the great faces we see are the ones that manifest sincerity, humility and grace when these faces are riding on the crest of the wave in the world around.   Another is the face we see not necessarily riding high, but one that exhibits a prevailing sense of the positives of life, and in the compelling process it spreads its influence around others in its company.   What goodness would come to the world if we had more and more of the faces of these people with dreams and triumphs of the greatness of life reflecting on their faces!

Do We Show Gratitude?

In many cases we could not do without the goodness we receive from others, even when we do or do not deserve all that we receive. The givers of goodness are kind, generous, bestowing and even friendly and loving. We believe that the givers are moved to do what they do, only because of their feelings, and maybe in appropriate cases because of their friendship and their love for us, and because of all that we represent to them.

We have received and continue to receive so much in terms of inner peace and of friendship, of love and of some material things. We have been in need in the distant past, in the immediate past. We will be in need in the future. We ourselves have given much to ourselves.

Many of us show our gratitude to those who approve of us, and manifest this approval in their kindness to us. Some of us do not extend our gratitude, negligently, deliberately or otherwise. At the receiving end of approval, of friendship, of love and good on our side, there is sometimes a thanklessness, an aloofness, a sense of unappreciative response, a reluctance to be expressive, an inability to manifest our gratitude. In a proper setting, it is frustrating to see that too many of us do not present a sincere and humble posture.

All this, or some of this, lack of gratitude may be unintentional. Some could be intentional, and yet some of it may flow from a nonchalant attitude. Regardless of the cause, lack of gratitude can be damaging in any relationship, particularly if the ingratitude persists, and the failure to express gratitude comes to the fore. In a relationship we must search around to see how we can remedy any damage that ingratitude or lack of proper gratitude may have inadvertently caused.

Ingratitude goes against the moral grain of most people. All of us must learn to be thankful to those who have done things for us or who continue to do things for us. We must be appreciative. We must be grateful. We must do this because this is what human relations, human behavior, and the richness of life are all about.

As humans we expect gratitude for the good we do. When we have earned it, we deserve it. We should always receive it. In the other role, we should always extend gratitude to others in a generous measure, in a sincere, becoming and thankful manner.

Be Wary

D o not begin or continue human relationships when you feel negative about certain people you meet or you know, or when you become suspect of their motives, their intentions. Nevertheless, to be wary of people, of events, and of things and situations around us is a facet of prudent living, more essential in today's society than ever before. We must maintain our composure, our vigilance and beef up our self-confidence. Our concentration on the task ahead of us must not be dimmed.

Unfortunately, there are those around us who seek to take advantage of others. They exploit every opportunity when they sense that somebody is weak or off-guard, or is not only sincere and honest, but is trusting and truthful and can be won over. These exploiters revel in the opportunities that lie before them.

We are not speaking of the evildoer who at a moment's notice jumps on his or her victim, attacking the person with physical violence and intensity, or causing bodily harm, despicable as these offenders are. We are speaking of the person who preys on the mind of another person, and takes the person unknowingly captive. The captive becomes the victim through a process of mind-play, even veiled language, and other deceptive methods.

These marauders will do things, say things and act in a manner that is most appealing to those soon to be made captive. The marauders have a plan in mind, a plan that may have been used by them before. The captive gets sucked in inch by inch, step by step. Mutual approval and, at times, a little admiration of the marauder grows on the victim. The captivator is generally a shrewd student of human nature, and senses progress and advancement in the battle plan he or she has hatched. The goal is unequivocally clear to the evildoers. Their intrigue and their design for battle are not faint or blurred to them. They have analyzed and dissected the thought process of their victim, and are playing on the victim's vulnerabilities. They gauge how weak their victims are. At times the captivators see their progress halted, or they see setbacks. They reassess the situation. They reinforce their resolve. They redouble their efforts. They might increase the bait to make it more appealing. If necessary, they alter their strategy and even their course of action. They are unconcerned about any public scorn. As time moves on, they become more vicious, and may be as strident as they feel meets their evil need. In the more extreme cases, they injure and they diminish their victims, and they can even deny these victims their life.

At times the intended victims can see the mischievous purpose of the evildoer, and can break off from the noose before they discover they may be irretrievably bound. At other times, the intended victims are drawn deeper and deeper into the fray. The captivators are skillful, and in their relations with each other they take measures that may be somewhat distasteful to the intended victim, or doubly appealing to the victim. Even though the intended victim may be at the final stage of the fray, he or she may have the chance to break away to freedom and in all clarity be able to understand how they have been ensnared.

The tragedy is when a good and decent person is in the all-enticing grip of the victimizer. The victimizer has denied the freedom of the victim, and through deceitful means has taken away much that is seen to be good in that person.

Much too often, in the final outcome, the evildoers overpower their intended victims. The perpetrators are unrelenting. They are self-trained to be persistent. They press hard to achieve their objectives. At times their evil is discovered early on. At other times the discovery is after the damage and the destruction are done. So, be wary of these evildoers operating in several fields of our society. If we are not on the alert, we can experience a poignant misunderstanding and we can experience more than a little grief.

We must maintain our composure and beef up our self-confidence. Our concentration on the tasks of life ahead, even perhaps a little hazy on the horizon, must not be dimmed. Let us remain vigilant and be wary of the evil around us in our society. Let us forever be on our guard. In our generation, the world has moved into too much of greed, malice, and prejudice. In Life we can have one crisis after another, and we should not ever relax our guard. Remember that to be wary is the right approach to life. To be wary and to remain protected from the evildoer have both the sense of fulfillment and of reward. This guard is not one-time, but everyday.

WITHOUT A CAUSE IN LIFE

A s we go about our everyday life, we encounter people who appear to be without direction, without purpose, without even as little as a minor goal in life. In certain sectors of society these people are few and far between. In other sectors of society they are not only quite a few, but in some respects they are a pervasive part of their society. They are not only aimless, with cynical pessimism attributed to them, but they are sad, depraved and dejected. They show no personal enthusiasm for even little in life. They display the symptoms of a monstrous enigma grabbing their life.

These are people who can be said to be a people without a cause in life. They do not live. They exist. They find no reason to live. They see no purpose in life. They have no cause in life, not even a personal ambition to live with a small degree of satisfaction, a small degree of success in the ordinary things of life. They are killing themselves with the prod of self-pity. They hurt those around them, particularly young children in their formative years. Some of these people exist without a murmur. Some rent and rave. They complain. They are bitter. Some carry outward signs of being tired in feeling helpless. They blame everyone else but themselves for their unhappy and unfortunate state. In most cases they have done little or nothing to travel the road out of their own decadence and misfortune. They choose to rather sit on the sidelines. They should know that their state of life is partly their own creation and is not to be flirted with.

They are in life without a cause. Even if they have been in this state for only a short while, they have been there too long. They lack the resolve to undo their past. They do not muster the mental strength or the courage to handle the situation. They do not see the dawn of a new day. They do not look for the rising sun on the horizon. They live in abject mental misery. They cannot bring themselves to make a new start. They remain afraid of delusion and immediate danger. Fear overwhelms them, even to do the very least to better their position. They lie back, trashed and humiliated. An element that enters into their thinking is envious resentment of other people in society, and this hampers and even destroys any efforts they attempt at making for a better life. They must recognize that anger is obstructive and can render them helpless and can become a bar to friendliness. They must put the past behind their warring attitude, and usher in a cooperating system of conduct.

Society through the medium of social organizations and religious organizations can and, at times, does enter the scene. Psychologists, counsellors and ministers of religion have a critical and constructive role to assume, and many of these have done much and are playing a fine role for those in need. It is not an easy task. It is not plain sailing in rocky waters. It is an uphill battle with open and placid resistance in its plenty. On occasion, the victims of their own doing are not only more arrogant, but they are physically and mentally aggressive. Every effort must be made to guide them in knowing where and how to begin, and how to grow out of their misery. Those who are working to help them out of their predicament and who are striving to give them a cause in life stand aghast at what they see in this branch of humanity. We should continue to encourage and help these fine people in these organizations in their difficult tasks.

The people without a cause in life can be a menace to society. By their presence and over time, they can destroy a larger and yet larger sector of society. Unfortunately, our community leadership and those around them do not seem to be able to do enough to cure a cancerous affliction. These victims are not only self-destructive, but they are drawing to the pit of disaster many of our younger generation.

Individually, we may not be able to cure all the damage in their life, but we can work collectively with them. It is an uphill fight, with, at times, little or no personal reward for those who venture to work with them. Nevertheless, those who can and want to work should give to all around them a positive cause in life; if not directly working with those in need, they should at least be setting an example of the beauty and the magnificence that can be created in life, once those who need to change direction set their course on the constructive avenues of life.

THE WORLD OF
FINE PEOPLE

I n everyday life we come across people who we respect, we honor, we admire, we befriend, we love. In addition to being with this group of people in our homes, we meet them at our work places, in schools and colleges, at church assemblies, and at our social gatherings. We see them on public transport, in stores and shopping malls, in the banks. They are at sports events and public entertainment sites, in hospitals and clinics, at bus and train stations, at airport boarding lounges. They are walking on the streets and in a host of other places where people mingle, or congregate or come across each other as they go about their worldly affairs.

The world of fine people greets people. They do so with feelings of courtesy and civility, with friendship and with good cheer. They enter into conversation, into discussion with those they want to. They give respect, they earn respect. They do things for others, often without the thought of receiving anything in return. When they do things for themselves, they do so with careful regard for and even special concern not to hurt others. The urge is to move in the direction of life in harmony. In their close circles, they know each one of us needs love when we are angered, when we are hurt.

They learn to welcome. They learn to befriend. They learn to admire. They are friendly in attitude, in expression and in conduct. They search for the superior qualities in others. They love to be with one or more of these fine people, some people much more than others. They are fed by an inborn and a cultivated companionship.

They break down barriers. They overlook their own human limitations and the limitations of those around. They tend to emphasize the goodness in others. Humility and self-effacement gain prominence within themselves. In time, they search to release others from their problems. They are there to reconcile differences. At times, they may lean over to make amends for others. They learn to comfort the less fortunate. They show empathy. They offer encouragement in difficult situations. They refrain from pronouncing judgements. They are compassionate towards others who are less fortunate. They forgive with grace when the need arises. They try not to hold back innovative concepts in their relations with others. They are receptive to newness in thinking. The posture they create is the goodness of genuineness and sincerity.

None of this is one-sided, or should it be one-sided. It takes two to do it all; it takes two to tango. In our human condition, we need another person or persons to love, to make life together, to respect, to honor, to befriend. We discover fulfillment for ourselves in the enrichment of the lives of those we come across and associate with, and in a special way, those we love. This is true in the inner family, as it is true in the world around us.

This world of fine people that we recognize and who recognize us make the universe a world of wonder for all of us to live in.   These fine people can get us closer to make the virtue of goodness permeate our life.   We are richer in life because of these fine people.   We are all fed by companionship. It is in this situation that, in our lifetime, friends sow many seeds of the good life.   We strive to gain a vivid vision of the joy of life from them.   All this is in the world of fine people. May this concept and reality of the world grow and grow, and may more and more of us become a part of the beauty of this world of fine people.

SOME OF OUR YOUNG TODAY

The young of today are our community's future, the national future, and in the larger context what the world will soon be in the immediate future and in generations to come. They will make our world. They can break our world. We honor the good amongst them. We applaud them in their efforts to be good and to do good. We encourage others who are not in this category today to become good, to lead constructive lives and to excel.

But yet in this world there is another side. Society is permeated by the not-so-good. In some areas the less good achieve dominance on the scene around us. Unfortunately, for this reason there is a propensity and a growing tendency to generalize and berate and condemn the young of today. The bad, perhaps unknowingly, rebuke the good among our young. At times, they almost blot out the good. When we speak of the young we mean the teenagers and the early twenties and maybe even a little older, and perhaps in certain situations the little more advanced. In this world around us today, there are bad elements that should do all they possibly can to transform and to reform themselves into human beings the world can discover joy in. But in all the young, there is a large number that we can be proud of, and those who need our support and our approval, all of whom should become more and more prominent and gain ascendancy on the community scene and on the national scene.

Let us select some from the group of the good. Each of the people we select is an example of and representative of the good. They are positive in their outlook on life. They conduct themselves conforming to the accepted standards. They perform achieving good, without causing harm or damage to others. They are cordial. They will not sell or trade the future for the present. They remain cool and debonair on the many lifestyles and diversity in people they see around them. They embrace and uphold their culture, diverse as other cultures may be from their own thinking. They are not diffident in their conduct.

Many issues in life are mysterious, perplexing and yet compelling. We see actions, reactions, interactions, counter-actions among the young. The good try not to speak anyone else's lines. We will dwell on just a few features of their life today. Education, training and intellectual betterment of self are not just among their high priorities; at times they are their single highest goal. They assign much time and effort in focusing on the future achievement of these aspects of their priority through the media of college classes, counselling classes, group sessions, seminars, books, recorded tapes and advancing technology. In sessions together, they at times extensively and in considerable detail will review each other's participation role, and engage in discussing the issues involved. The power of the written word, the power of the spoken word become paramount. Those who have achieved in this, are now prepared to move on to successful careers and soon find themselves on the path of growth and advancement.

Some of the young are not churchgoers. It is disappointing that at times we see the non-practice of religion in them as rather unusual and uncommon for their position in life, their age group, and the influences that impact them. We know some of them have proper religious tendencies, and that their nonreligious pattern can change in a relatively short time.

There are just as many of the young who are openly supportive of the religious attitude and the deep religious beliefs and practices in their community. Some will even speak about religion, sparked by their interest in and their inherent and expressed love for their Creator. They will enter into a dialogue on faith and the fervent belief in the greatness and the omnipotence of God. They recognize that religion is a lighthouse for their growth and progress and that it remains in the vicinity of their life to enter port and to anchor themselves for a while and more before they sail on.

We will pause to look at the not-so-good in society today. Pain and misery are sadly part of their life. Some of this may have originated from a breakdown in family life. Self-respect in all its intensity and depth have not been encouraged. They are trapped by conflicting pulls. They have been vulnerable to peer pressure. Their outlook, their attitudes, their points of view are defined primarily by those with whom they associate. There is intimidation in their lives. There is sheer indulgence. We see a lack of passion and compassion. They have been challenged. Ideological attitudes have not taken root in them. They find themselves unable to address constructively the thorny questions of right and wrong. Life is a demanding journey for them. They should not be weighed down by where they are now. They should not be influenced in the negative. In their own mind, society, lifestyles, ethics, politics, religion and more leave them helpless. Not all of us in any age group can agree amongst ourselves in these critical areas of life, and controversies and conflicts arise. But we all have to take a stand, hopefully a stand that hurts no one, not even ourselves in our great need.

The world has been witness to a revolution among certain people, particularly those who have brought to life no desire to be achievers in life. They have grown adamant. They feel directed and condemned. They find themselves at a stage helpless in situations where they do want to be good people, productive people and a credit to society. We are witnesses of the hopelessness into which some of them have sunk. Some even show in their attitude that they do not have to contribute to their own lives, one iota of the good that is in others and the good that could be with them and in them.

We see bad sexual revolutions in many ways, in many facets of life. We see homelessness, poverty and a life to do nothing. Life is barren for them. We see the abandonment of all human effort to progress as part of their public character. More of our people should work to bring in all haste their innermost pain and torture to organizations, groups, family and individuals who can and will aid them. A class of intellectuals in all endeavors can be born amongst them. They have to learn to pull in the reins. Impulsiveness for a life of achievement should be within their battle cry.

We must have our ailing youth in all age groups recapture the spirit of good decent living, born of the spirit of enterprise. If they pursue the search, they can have so much on their side. The world owes them everything for a good life, and in some respects the world owes them nothing, unless they work to create the good in their life.

Our young are our jewels today. For ages, they have always been so. In the world around, the young who are great and have been great should move on to even greater accomplishment. They have a mission in life. They are a marvel and a store of our treasure which we should never surrender. We are proud of them and will always be, and we hope that many, many more will join their ranks. The not-so-young in society should not fail in becoming to the young the beacons for greatness and for achievement.

10.07

People, Cultures and Lifestyles

T he term Race in a particular context denotes a pre-birth classification and an unchangeable affiliation for all time. It designates humankind into divisions with specific characteristics of skin pigmentation, and some facial and bodily traits and tendencies. For centuries the passage of time has not changed significantly any of this, and it has not seen humanity's characteristics replaced with pure, undiluted universal ethnicity. In all probability, the world cannot and will not. It may not change ever. The white have remained white, the brown, brown, the yellow, yellow, the black, black and there are those who manifest more than one racial origin. Then, in addition, distinctions among people emanate from history buried in the distant past and in the not-so-distant past, from geographical facets, from folklore and from lifestyles dictated to them or lived by them and their ancestors. There are also differences coming from human values, from language, social horizons, patterns and attitudes, economic values, sexual preferences and from life's customs and practices. In some countries, immigration at one stage or another has infused a strong international mix into ethnicity.

When we travel around the world and see humanity in its diversity of ethnic people, their differing characteristics, their conduct, their poise, their good and their evil, we take time to sit back and ponder over the heterogenous nature of humanity. The people we see, and the people we meet present us with an interesting, and at the same time, an intriguing assembly of genetics in humanity. The reality of ethnology strikes us in its bare, alarming form, captivating our attention and perhaps questioning our understanding of humanity. Our presumptions come under review. The interrogating of us on our assumptions embedded in ageless time is brought to the fore. Before us is spread the conflict of cultures, symbols, beliefs and attitudes. We see the efforts made to overcome the least admitted conflicts, the ancient rituals, the hatred and the anger that has plagued humanity for so long.

We are in the same life span and even in the same society as these people, but we come together with different cultures and not the same ethnic origins, with different backgrounds, different family values and codes, different age emphases on life. We experience the contrasts between civilizations. We come together with, maybe, not even the same educational and economic backgrounds and not the same life achievement goals. It need not be a humbling experience, but it can be when we do not speak or, maybe, even will not speak or understand each other's native language. This is particularly true when one side or both sides cannot communicate in a more universal language.

Ethnic life patterns can be very set, but they are not unchangeable. For many people cultures influence our life patterns and affect our philosophy and psychology. Ethnicity gives rise to attitudes, habits, leanings, beliefs and prejudices.

Our cultures have an effect on our behavior, on our adopted and adapted affiliations and on our thinking. Ethnicity can affect our sense of loyalties, our leanings and our priorities on life's path.

People have their good points and their not-so-good points, some of these aspects more dominant than others. The roots of some of these elements are embedded in history. In one's own human frailties and limitations, one cannot understand the plan or fathom the wisdom that gave the world this racial distinction in people, with an ethnicity that is the diversity, the origin and the cause of some of the advantages of each ethnic people and at the same time the origin and the cause of so much conflict, division, hatred and anger among people. When all else leads to the unification of the human race, ethnicity and only a few religions remain obstinately but very openly the non-conforming, the separating, the distancing and the antagonizing influence on people. We cannot alter trends, and we must live with them or ignore them as appropriate.

Now to turn to another aspect. The Supreme Being not only created the human race, but he brought into being the Magnificence and the Wonderment of Nature and of Humanity. What Magnificence and Wonderment it is and has been! Let us give thought to this for a moment. We are the people who should promote harmony between people on all fronts. We should guard against discrimination on the bases of race, ethnicity, religion, culture, age, sex, sexual preference and language to name some of the barriers too many of us erect against harmonious living.

Despite all this Magnificence and Wonderment, ethnic groups have for centuries remained largely apart, each in their own particular habitation. In the past century or two and a little more, changes have come about because of migration. The process of change is continuing, and proceeding to develop more rapidly in the second half of this century. The changes have been a blessing. In most continents and in many countries, a melting pot of races has developed, and development is accelerating whenever political entities have sanctioned migration to their countries or have unwittingly allowed it to happen. Friendships have taken root, and so have dislike, animosity and hatred among people.

At times one ethnic group has been fearful and suspicious of the other. The unnecessary conflict of opposing cultures is the cause of some of this. We see layers upon layers of prejudice. There is poverty. There is ethnic disharmony. We discuss the rebellious nature of people. Let us hope that before long in the next century, fear and suspicion and hatred, and even dislike will be largely eradicated from relationships between different ethnic people. We all have a part to play. We all have to work toward the goal of goodwill and brotherhood and sisterhood among all people. We have to search for avenues that are conducive to growth and advancement.

National leaders and community level leaders in some countries and in some ethnic groups have themselves not done enough to disavow hatred of other races. They have not encouraged effectively and in all sincerity their own people to banish ethnic differences and to treat all people as one. We all have to correct the wrongs in our own sector of society. We can move as individuals, we can move as groups, as communities. Community and national leaders are sometimes our drawback, because they have the power to encourage and work for unification, but they may not have acted constructively and they may not have done enough. We all have to win the respect and the friendship of others. This cannot happen if our thoughts take abode in an offensive and aggressive attitude, and our actions and conduct portray the negative. The younger generation are in a quandary when they see their leaders take the stand of what is popular, not a stand on what is right. Society is today plagued with this class of damaging leadership at several levels. The young should lead a peaceful rebellion in a constructive and positive way against nonperforming leadership.

Civility and proper conduct have declined in world society, more in some countries than in others. The decline must stop and all civility and proper conduct should be promptly built and restored. The world was so different fifty years and more ago. From nation to nation, cultures were diverse and distinct. In some cases with the passage of time the distinctions have become less pronounced. Racism, whether it be from brown, yellow, white or black is sometimes used as a crutch for our own personal and individual deficiencies, for our shortcomings and the lack of the basics of life. Mixing among peoples and the process of immigration have more than moved people closer together. In the past twenty years the world has changed. There is greater acceptability of one racial group by another, but this acceptability is not total or at times not sufficient, either for groups or for individuals.

The younger generation has seen momentous changes. Some of the young are on a perilous journey. Twenty years ago life's priorities were different, attitudes were different, sophistication was different. Ambitions were distinct from one ethnic partition and one cultural partition to another. The goal and the approach now taking root or in existence amongst people are hopefully a blend of the best of all worlds. An overriding vision of hope must take possession of more and more of our world. The younger generation must become increasingly aware that one cause of disparity in economic attainment is the one that flows largely many a time from our own personal approach to achievement and perseverance in the right direction.

Too few people, even the minority that they are, project in their conduct an awareness beyond their own race. They are to be complimented. But there are too many people harboring personal hurt, their personal inadequacy with and personal jealousy of others. They exhibit imaginary pride and greatness. The latter are to be ignored, and discreetly despised. We hope that the number of good people will grow rapidly, and that their input and their influence will spread more rapidly.

As different racial groups inter-marry, our native cultures will fade away and disappear, but racial hatred and prejudice may not. Any significant change in this area may not happen until well into the twenty-first century. Cross-cultural issues surface. Native cultures can be positive, they can be negative. Unfortunately cultures can become extinct when younger generations ignore their ancestry. Cultures are not shallow, even when they seem shallow. If we are not on our guard, we will lose reminders of our heritage. This is regrettable. The creation of peace and harmony is to be promoted in the proper context and at the proper level. Ancestral pride and achievement are to remain on an equal, not necessarily in the background. In a positive vein everything should be done to retain our heritage, but it must not dominate the scene, particularly in a negative tone.

Ethnocentrism can be damaging to human relations. For egocentrics it defines, often erroneously, that one's own ethnic group is superior to other ethnic groups. Prejudice based on race is not new, and has been on the world scene for centuries. Separatism and pride in race are characteristics in some people. Their thinking can have its drawbacks. The unwise and the not-so-wise act on this notion and do colossal damage to themselves and to the world.

Some people stigmatize individuals in other ethnic groups. A rival gathering of people tends to revile those who seek to promote harmony. The good in the group are branded with the bad, for the only reason that they are members of the derided ethnic group, taunted by those who brand them. We have all to develop in the direction that no one is to be credited or discredited on the basis of his or her race. Society must decry racism in its negative implications. Society must acclaim individuals regardless of their race. For the positive and the constructive elements, the call should go out to bring together people of different races, different customs and lifestyles, different languages and different religions. This is but one way to build human harmony, regardless of differences.

Racial, religious, cultural and economic differences should not be the decision factors. People are black and are regal. People are yellow, brown and white and they are regal. They can all be regal in the worldly sense. The assembly of not the same races, not the same heritage, different languages, different religions and different ways of life should not be destructive. On the contrary, all this can be made to be positive and constructive.

Our pronounced ethnic identity, our diverse backgrounds and cultures and our specific characteristics must not become divisive. On the contrary, we someways can and someways we cannot value one another from our differences. We cannot change ethnicity, however much we want to do this. Let us learn to accept individuals on the basis of their being a particular individual person, without any attention to their racial origin. Every day that this is done by more and more people, every day will the world and our own world around us be a better place for all to live in.

Merging of lifestyles has contributed, has helped immensely in promoting harmony. In some nations including the world's lead nations, some old cultures remain largely intact, and in a few cases have become more intensified with the passage of time. We must begin by accepting that we are all different, from our ethnic origin and as individuals. Do not curse our differences. Do not decry our differences. We should all respect each other's ethnicity, not one being superior or inferior to another. In a certain way, celebrate our differences as this approach becomes appropriate or pertinent. To judge or to misjudge by appearance should not be inherent in our society.

As we stand on the threshold of the new millennium, the elements of race, religion, language and origin must not remain in the forefront to the extent that these elements remain in prominence and remain as confrontational issues, even though so many of us may not admit this. The resultant damage in not following the positive course is inestimable. There are many unexplained webs in this world. In the world today, there is one fear, and that is that race, religion and culture can become a rapidly growing obsession.

Ethnic cleansing should not become prevalent in any regions of the world. Even today, as we approach the twenty-first century, some racial conflicts gain ascendancy in the process of living. Be mindful of this drawback. Be proud of your culture. Take pride in your ethnic background, and promote interracial harmony. More can be done at the local levels to cure the ills of disharmony. Social interaction must be encouraged. Let us not suppress or banish native culture in any ethnic background. Let us learn to respect the diversity of people, and by our example work for the inclusiveness of all people. Work on the basis that the existence of ethnicity will not be damaged or destroyed by time, but that each of us can introduce and promote the positives of race. Be proud of your race, your history, your religion, your upbringing, your place in society, and in all this take pride in the way in which you treat and respect others of all racial, ethnic and cultural origin.

MAKE BYGONES
A TREASURE

REMEMBER THAT DAY WHEN......

A ll around us are memories filled with wonder and thrill, and, we hope, with the least of disappointments, denials and sadness. Memories are a significant aspect of life, and we should preserve them, treasure them in the proper context. Let us venture back along the path of life, for in this exercise we will experience a dramatic revelation of the theme of time. In some ways the path is clear and the visibility is good, and the recall can be vivid. In others, the range of mental vision is cloudy and misty, and recollection has faded or is dim and is receding.

We will begin with that Day When......

You were a child, good most of the time but naughty, adventure-filled and bad some of the time. This was and is natural for a child, and is very much commonplace in growing up.

You recall the wonder of your parents and of other members of the family. You bring back to mind all the good they gave you and all the good they did for you in all situations, difficult as the positions might have been.

As you were growing up, you got the feel of and experienced some of the wonders of the world and of the people who were around you.

Your school days gave you exposure to many interesting aspects of life. You made friends, and you liked some people more than you liked or did not like others.

Remember that Day When......

The academic and extracurricular activity successes during your student days gave you a strong anticipation of triumph and of the glory of life. Educational and training awareness properly took abode in you. You were at a stage in life when at times you resorted to denying the limitations in your life, however few or many they may have been.

You pursued your training and your study to the stage of graduation in school and in college. You stood poised to begin your working life. You decided on a career, or found yourself in the vicinity of a career exploration.

You chose to participate in the opportunities, few at times, before you.

At this juncture, you became more aware of the existence of an intellectual quandary in the expanse of life. You began to understand the conflicting tugs and pulls in life.

Remember that Day When......

You accepted your first career-employment, and in doing this, you perceived a more intense tremble and anxiety within you. You learned that this experience was not uncommon.

Your early career had some major jolts, which were unsettling and at times perplexing.

As you moved on, you had more than a few, maybe many

accomplishments. These were successes that brought you a feeling of the majesty of life.

You continued from one achievement to another and another, winning deserved acclaim from family and friends. You saw that the person who blinked first was the loser. You became aware that the dawn of youth was fleeting by.

Remember that Day When......

You began to feel an attraction to the person with whom would in time develop endearment and mutual love, love that would be to last forever. You gave this person the gift of attention, and this person gave you the attention that became reciprocal. Soon after, romance was communicating itself, and commitment was developing and love would flourish.

You both dreamed about what each of you wanted in each other, and you both followed your dreams. The burning desire of caring very much for each other had taken root.

You realized that you had not been friends with anyone else with the sensibility and the love that you and your hoped for life-partner-to-be had manifested. As the love between you and your loved one blossomed and grew, the miracles of life in their own special way began to attain their peak.

In time, you married your love, and the glory of life shone forth in all its splendor.

You prayed that your honeymoon with all its love and glamour would never end. Today you recall how you have been blessed.

Remember that Day When......

Your first-born came into the world in a babe's total innocence and beauty, with no worldly concerns.

Each of your children added to the joy and the happiness of the family, each in their own unique way and with special characteristics all their very own.

The children advanced in their education and training and in their careers, and they built on their early foundation.

The children married. They went their own distinguishing ways, maintaining their relationships with you. They always wanted you to partake of all their newfound joy, and to be part of their lives.

The children grew in age and in wisdom, and we became proud of who they had created of themselves.

Remember that Day When......

You celebrated each of your birthdays and each of your anniversaries amidst feelings of accomplishment over the years and conscious of the challenge of the years to come.

You celebrated achievements of each member of the family, be these in school, in their career, in their family life, in the sports arena, in public life and in all walks of life.

Remember that Day When......

You had the gnawing feeling of some awareness of what the advancing and changing pattern of life now called for and would call for, and even demand from us, in the future, at times without attention to our own selections.

You learned that most people are not spared sad experiences. You saw that success is denied to those not informed, those not in command, those not in control. In the midst of your inabilities and your inadequacies, this particular success was given to others.

Failure, disappointment, illness and tragedy took toll of

you and fear overcame you. The roaring depth of insecurity took possession of you. There was little veiled in front of you. You recalled that you were once told that you could not plan in advance for some crises. For any of this, there could be no rehearsals, no trials, no practice sessions.

You experienced that it was wiser not to avenge an insult, even when there was emotional damage within you. The damage within you had to be contained and even suppressed, and you would have to be the person to do this. You learned that after the pain came the healing, and that the healing could be like a miracle.

At times, life seemed so forlorn, so hollow and so empty, and God seemed to forsake you, but you knew that God had the almighty power to restore order from chaos. You were confident that God would come to the rescue if you only asked for this blessing in all loyalty and in all faith. In our own life, we, the people, made God visible or invisible for ourselves.

Despite all these happenings, you did not fail to thank God in all sincerity for his goodness to you, and for the miracle of shielding you from greater difficulties and more severe and unending misfortunes. You acknowledged that God has been and will remain in the detail of your life.

Remember that Day When......

You became more fully aware that most successes had perhaps many attendant challenges, and that compulsive individuality should remain in the forefront. You saw the need at different intervals in your life for a redefinition of your guideposts in much of your involvement.

You saw that in many structures in life, there were three

sides — the individuals involved, the conflicting issues, and the immediate and the future concerns of all.

In certain situations in order to accommodate for your own good and for the good of others, you had to compromise yourself and your thinking, and, at times, your actions and the level of your performance.

You sensed an identity crisis, at times at the most critical phases in your life. There had to be some refashioning of your goals and of your activity in order for you to attain achievement.

You did not want your personality to overshadow originality, merit and substance.

In real life around you, you saw more readily the illusion of success and happiness being coupled with the background of wealth and affluence. You saw a few people overwhelmed by their intellectual success.

Remember that Day When......

You sat there grim and forlorn, and mourned at your plight, refusing to search for the silver lining in the cloud beyond. Your now confused thinking began to take its toll. But you did not permit loneliness, solitude and denial to take charge of your life.

You nearly despaired in all this array of shattered hopes and dreams, but you did not submit to abandonment. You sat back and pondered, and then a glimmer of hope reached you through your own strengths and, at times, the encouraging counsel of a friend.

A person reached out to you, and there began a bond of trust, and of respect that required both parties to give and to receive, if this new field of friendship was to expand and develop. In your lifetime, you came across more and more of this category of good people.

You saw the urgency to banish from life's patterns all excuses for failures and inadequacies. You knew that after every storm, every blizzard, would come the calm.

Remember that Day When......

You were persuaded to do things you did not want to do or you were inclined not to do, but despite this message, couched at times in a warning, you did what you did. You had felt that you could sometimes live by your wits.

You began to see laid before you the unfailing truth of the message that with God nothing is impossible. You were convinced that God was inextricably woven in your own life, and that we are never alone if we ask God to remain always with us.

You became aware that it is tragic to lose God and not know or even come to a realization of the loss.

You acknowledged that there is no dress rehearsal for many of the significant events in real life.

At times, you may have sung a little off-key, at times again with little melody or rhythm in your life song, but these performances by you on life's scene did not harm your life. For you, these were not the only opportunities to perform.

Remember that Day When......

You had made mistakes, and you learned from them. You learned from the mistakes of others. You comforted yourself that you did not want to make the mistakes they had made. You had much to learn from those around you, and to grow in prudence and in wisdom.

You saw the many positives in your life. You gained knowledge from the past and from the present. You learned for the future yet to be laid before you. In your thinking, in your deliberations, in your debate with others around, no concept pertaining to the activity remained irrelevant.

You saw yourself in a fortress that you built to ensure that it could not be penetrated by evildoers. There were times, when you had a vision or more beyond attainment, even a vision beyond human limitations.

You believed in togetherness, away from isolation. People knew that you would respond in a certain way, and people could be confident of the outcome.

We will break at this stage. Thus far, we have proceeded to do some, maybe not all the recalls in our life. In all these recalls, there are happenings we want to remember. There are happenings we want to remember, but we cannot. In this we sometimes find one of the most humbling of the realities of life. In addition, there are things which we can recall, but we would rather have them banished from our mind. In certain situations, nostalgia can be comforting, it can be consoling.

Unless we are prepared to sit back and recall the past, life can be likened to a glacier in the Arctic Circle, several of which we have seen and we have admired, and we learn that only a bare tenth of the glacier is visible to the human eye. Nine-tenths is out of sight below the water surface. In our recall, this scene is real and alive for us if we have been to the glaciers and if we have been present, gazing and watching this unforgettable beauty of nature. There is the visible, the not visible, the less visible, the less obvious. This pattern can be very much like your life and my life.

We recognize that life has glory, majesty, success and triumph. We also recognize that life has disappointments, sadness, sorrow, failures and damage-repair. There is so much to remember in life, not only the agonies and the ecstasies. There is so much that is good, and all this not only contributes, but makes for the enchantment of life. But in all this, we must guard against getting immersed in Time. We must Remember that Day When............, and, hopefully, the goodness of life for you and for me will go on, the goodness of life will grow and grow.

A TIME TO CELEBRATE

The milestones on Life's journey are not counted in years, or in the distance that separates each of them. Milestones are not equidistant. Milestones do not come on life's scene only once a year, but they come sometimes more often or less often in any one year. They mark our spectacular triumphs, our discomforting setbacks, our joyous episodes and our sad events. They are the beacons for major adjustments in our thinking and in our action and reaction. They make for the resetting of our course on our passage through life. A new strategy is to be mapped out. As we journey along, we pray that most of our future milestones in life may emerge from among our finest investment in purpose, in time and in effort.

As we have said before to ourselves, in our early years, what we are is God's gift to us. As we journey along, what we become is our gift to God. As we look around, we can see what a splendid gift many are making to our Creator. Each milestone makes its mark for all to see.

In matters that affect us, there are decisions we make and there are decisions we do not make. We need guidance, including much self-guidance. We should work from properly based conclusions. We need direction in the hard decisions we have to make for ourselves, sometimes decisions affecting relations and friends, and even affecting those who are not our friends. When decisions are made out of conviction to enrich our life and without intent to hurt others, we live true to self. Friendship is a two-way street. What a great friend we can be! In all this, you may have to refashion the path of your dreams. Even in the darkest hours, always seek the silver lining that lies in wait beyond. We will continue to reach the milestones of our Life. In the process, do nothing that will hurt others.

Life should not only be measured in years. What would you do if you could get your time back on life's journey? On your birthday sit back for a moment, and feel good, hopefully very good, about yourself. Take a close look at yourself. You are very special. The mystique about you can be compelling, unquenchable and all-embracing. On your birthday, reinforce your resolve to live to the highest ideals you have always searched for and worked for. Your birthday is a time of recall, and a time to celebrate.

The prayers on a friend's birthday and on our birthday are for joy, happiness, success and blessing in all endeavors. From time to time we give our friends a glimpse of the intrinsic beauty that lies within us. Give them a journey into some of your past. May we always be as splendid and as very special in our person and in our spirit as our friends know us. Our prayers are that we will be blessed always.

Let us celebrate our day by recalling our milestones on life's journey. With all the past milestones already in place, and with new milestones yet to come on the journey, we can and we should write our autobiography, not this time with our pen, but with our thoughts and our actions, and all that we do and all that goes on in our own life. This autobiography is special for our own little world and, maybe, for the bigger world to see. With the dawning of every morning begins a new day on life's journey, a new day of opportunity, a new day of adventure and, in this, on some days we encounter the less desired which we may not be able to avoid.

Make everyday a day for us to celebrate. Enjoy our successes. Milestones in life are precious. Some can be dazzling. They are ours forever. Again, some milestones can enrich our thinking, while others can impoverish us. We can become more sensitive to our own imperfections. Each of both these categories in milestones can be a brief stop in time for us to deliberate upon. Let us celebrate our life as often as we can, and let us be surrounded by all the happiness we can.

At The End of The Day......

A t the end of the day when all is done and nightfall descends on us, we would like an opportunity to pause, to sit back, to ponder, and to begin a process of assessment. We want to do this before we fall asleep, because just preceding sleep we expect that with our eyes shut we will be listening to the gentle sound of the waves as they break on our shores. The question that looms before us is: "What was all that happened today?"

The Day may have raced by with little or no opportunity to reflect on happenings until the end of the day. The day may have not been fast-paced. We often do not have the time to relive in our memory the day to any overall extent. But there are selected events in our path we stop to reflect upon. We begin the day's recall.

For many people every day is different. For many it is substantially the same as earlier days. For some today can be a replay of yesterday or earlier days. One hopes that on most days, if not every day, the good outweighs the not-so-good. But in the realities of life, we have to learn to accept that there is much bad and evil around. We need to be sheltered, or we need to develop the capability to weather the storms and to experience the calm and win.

Each day can be different. There are nights when with feelings of pride and a sense of quiet jubilation, we dwell on the successes and the triumphs of the day, sometimes the expectations from earlier times now fulfilled. We rejoice in these sentiments. Even if nothing big was achieved today, we derive happiness from all having gone well.

There are days when with feelings of disappointment, of sadness and perhaps, of fear, we think of the failures of new ventures and of continuing projects. We dwell on the lowered expectations of the outcome of projects in progress, the rescue missions to resuscitate what was started and what had moved or had not moved along.

Then again, there are days when with feelings of humility, reverence and gratitude we rejoice at what we have been endowed with. We look around and see the experience and the plight of those less fortunate, those who have been through catastrophic happenings. As we lie down at the end of the day, we recognize we have been blessed in terms of peace, rest and quiet. We stop and thank God for his goodness to us.

We are not without our days when with a seizure of trepidation, but hopefully at the same time a feeling of confidence in our ability to triumph, we visualize what lies before us. With the coming dawn of the next day, we form our own mental images in terms of work, of challenges, problems, unwanted chores and seemingly insurmountable situations. We attempt to give all these areas human dimensions.

We rapidly move to conclude our dialogue with our inner self. We feed ourselves on what we rejoiced in today. We see the successes, the triumphs, the good and all the fine people we associated with. Perhaps, we started a new friendship.

Unhappily, we have to face the less happy moments of the day. As part of our life, we have the bad, the ugly, the frustrations, the tortures, the hostile, the indifferent. We have had the confrontational, the vindictive, the hypercritical, the contradictory. We have had these choices in people and in events. We conclude that the results could have been worse, much worse. Hopefully, all these are overshadowed by the good, the beautiful, the successes, the rejoicing and the triumphs of the day. We are grateful for all that we achieved.

Let us stop in our review of our day. The past is once more behind us. We cannot undo the less favorable. We want to go forward, and not go backward. We do not want to be bogged down in the past. We want to rise from the rubble, little as it hopefully is. We are self-evidently comfortable with ourselves. The future lies ahead for us. Let us journey on, even when we know that the morrow may bring us to a new crossroad, perhaps a point, or more than one point of new decisions. Let us seek new strength, new resolve. We are different from what we knew about ourselves in the past. We are not the same. We will not be intimidated by anyone or by anything. How we rejoice when we know that the best days of our life are yet to be! We thank God. We direct our prayer to God. We are at the end of this day. Our conscious self dims and fades away into deep slumber. We shut our eyes. Soon we vanish into the magic and the elegance of the night.

WALK DOWN
MEMORY LANE

Memory Lane is on our life map, brightly lit and resilient. It has so much imprinted on it. So much, we hope, we would love to view as we journey along, and again, we hope, some we would not like to see, but it is there.

As we travel along, nostalgia can be comforting and it can be energizing, and, at times, maybe a little distressing. We have been brushed by scars in our confrontations in life. Distress and anguish have been astride in our path. We do not want to see the wreckage, regardless of its origin or its cause. Without always admitting our anguish, we defiantly affirm our dignity.

In Memory Lane we scan the horizon, and concentrate on the radiance of our accomplishments. These have been many. These have been great. We have had varying sources of support. We have not, we hope, lived in isolation. We have seen ourselves grow in love. We have grown in worldly wisdom. We have grown in gratitude. We want to banish anything that can be but an anticlimax to the positives in our life. We learn to draw more from our worth and from our value.

We have made dents in the life around us, some small, some with good, positive impact. We have made a difference. We have created a lifestyle for ourselves. We have confirmed that little, very little, can be obtained for little or for nothing. We have learned that the more forthcoming we are, the more we can influence how captive or receptive we can be to life's old philosophy or to life's new thinking.

As we walk along in Memory Lane, we must recognize that we should not get lost in the sands of time. At times, there emerges in life a conflict between image and substance. We acknowledge that we have made mistakes, some of them more than once. We sometimes wish we could be in our late teens again. Despite this, our Memory Lane must remain lighted, beaming brightly with lights. The brightness must not be shaded unduly or unnecessarily. The lessons of our life must endure. Our Memory Lane must remain monumental within our own life. We must always believe in being a winner. Without an attitude geared to winning, we cannot and will not win. Let us make each day a better and a better day than the day before and better than our earlier days.

WE ARRIVE AT
ONE DESTINATION

We Arrive at
One Destination

We stop in our path. We disembark for now. We have reached one destination. For us and for some fellow-travelers, this could have been a long journey. For some it could have been a not-so-long journey. All the same, it has been a journey, little planned, with the scenario and its expanse unknown at the start. Nonetheless, we have come to the end on this particular travel.

Some of us have now got additions to our baggage. In our disembarking baggage could be lodged the increasing acquaintance and the heightened familiarity we may have now gained with our own real life and the life of some of humanity. There can be much wrapped in our minds. We have observed some parallels in our own lives and in the lives of others. We have made discoveries. We have had glimpses into another person's and several other persons' life adventure. We may not agree with all that has been narrated to us on this journey, but we have earned an experience and possibly more than one insight that can be and will have impact on and be of some influence in our own life.

We have learned that life itself on its own cannot give us

happiness and cannot give us glory unless we really want most or all sectors of both, and above all we stand convinced that we must work for our goals. Life provides us the undefined vacuum in space, and, if we are so motivated, it is we who can fill the vacuum, and extend and extend what we have achieved. We reinforce our thinking that there is a bitter sweet price to pay for glory. We know that there is a long way to go. We know that much of the glory of life can be within our grasp. We know that there can be a long road to travel. Even if there is much more to be achieved, we should not be disheartened, we should not look down on ourselves, we should not look back at failures we may have experienced.

In our own unique way, as we go around abounding in life, we can all become a masterpiece, sacred, beautiful and growing in the wisdom of the world. When we reach the mountaintop, we hope that the moment of glory will prevail, and we pray, will last forever. Let us not lose faith in ourselves as we battle to get to the mountaintop, or to stay at the mountaintop. You and I may not be there yet. You and I may not have been there before. You and I may have some way to go. You and I have had some stumbles. The ascent to the top is steep. We see slippery slopes. The course may not be easy. Nevertheless, none of the drawbacks should discourage us. The failures, the disappointments should not hinder us. We should not live in excuses.

This is your life and it is my life, and our one and only life. We will not have another life. In your life and in my life, this section of the journey is but a milestone, not the end of our quest. Let us make each milestone one of emboldening significance. Let us brace ourselves and work to make each day better in every respect, armed with high resolution and with confidence built in ourselves. We can make our life a world of glory and a world of triumph for ourselves. It is you and I who can do this. Let us journey on in the Search for Life's Glory, even when there is a Sense of Life's Pain .....

ABOUT THE AUTHOR

Maurice Gracias was born in Nairobi, Kenya. He is a native of Goa, a small country that was then Portuguese territory on the subcontinent of India. Maurice is an economics graduate having completed his studies with European universities. Later, he was admitted as a Fellow of the Royal Economic Society in London, England. As an economist and a financial executive, he has functioned for many years on the national scene and the international scene in twenty countries. He has worked for and with national governments and organizations and with international bodies, including the United Nations, the World Bank, the United States Foreign Service, the British colonial service, and the European Economic Community. His early career was with the multi-mode British-developed and British-operated transportation system extending into three countries in East Africa. It was in the transportation finance system that Maurice was recognized by the British Government for his work, and was the first non-Britisher in East Africa relatively early in his career to be granted super scale officer status. In the professional arena, he has been associated with leaders at upper levels in various national governments and organizations, including participation in world congresses and White House conferences. He has worked with senior corporate leaders in several companies, including serving on the board of directors of an insurance company which he founded with other executives. He has been appointed to the Board of Regents of a leading U.S. organization. He has participated extensively in world sports and has won international acclaim in field hockey and in cricket. Serious illness forced his withdrawal from the final selection of the Kenya national field hockey team for the Melbourne Olympic Games in 1956.

Maurice has been keynote speaker at international conventions, and he has been lecturer on international and national economic issues and personal financial and estate planning in the United States and in other countries.

Maurice has lived in, worked in or traveled to more than sixty sovereign countries in every continent of the globe. He has been recognized by resolution of the California State Legislative Assembly as an outstanding immigrant to the United States. He has been distinguished through inclusion of his life story in worldwide biographical books in England, in the United States and in India.

In the course of his life and his work and his travels, Maurice has had many unique and perhaps unrivalled challenges in relating to people in different segments of society. These people have been from several racial and ethnic backgrounds, many cultures, many lifestyles and different life sectors. In these ethnic backgrounds and their subdivisions, Maurice has encountered people manifesting in the processes of life a wide spectrum of human situations and socioeconomic scenarios, a diversity of political persuasions and a range of religious convictions, all these so varied and in contrasts from one country to another, and from one society to another.

Through all this, Maurice's life has been enriched by these many experiences. He remains convinced that humanity is magnificent. In this book are portrayed some of his attempts to translate his world experiences into the contextual reality of life.